Life
Is a Do-Over

You Can Choose
a New Path in Life!

Cindy Clemens

First edition 2005
ISBN 0-9710696-5-4
978-0-9710696-5-7
Library of Congress Control Number: 2005934222
Printed and bound in the U. S. A.

10 9 8 7 6 5 4 3 2 1

Life Is a Do-Over
by Cindy Clemens

Published by Jorlan Publishing
Book and Cover Design by Jill Ronsley
www.JorlanPublishing.com

Cover Illustration © by Paula Tarver-Leckey
www.artzest.net
Back Cover Photo by Sandra Ballard

Dedicated to my incredible husband, Jim Clemens.

*Your unwavering love and support
have been the foundation for all of my work.
Thanks for being so willing to try new adventures,
and for showing me how to enjoy the ride each and every day.*

You truly are the wind beneath my wings.

Contents

Conclusion

Appendix One

Appendix Two

Introduction
Imagine Getting a Do-Over for Your Life

It is never too late to be what you might have been.

—George Eliot

While organizing my thoughts for this book, I took a break to watch one of my favorite movies, *City Slickers*. The story is about Mitch, played by Billy Crystal, who goes on a real cattle drive with his childhood buddies Ed and Phil, played by Bruno Kirby and Daniel Stern. The underlying story shows how each man admits to and resolves his mid-life crisis, then discovers what is most important in his life—his number one thing.

During one particularly revealing scene, Phil breaks down sobbing, admitting to his friends that he has lost his wife and his job and feels as though he has wasted his life. It is a very poignant moment. Mitch hugs his despondent friend and asks if he remembers when they played baseball as kids. If the ball got stuck in a tree, all they had to do was yell "do-over." This meant the hitter could hit the ball again—a free second chance. Phil gets a smile on his face, and Mitch reminds him that life is a do-over; he can have a clean slate to choose again. Phil takes this to heart, and by the end of the movie, we see a new Phil with a smile on his face and the beginnings of a much better life.

When I watched this scene, I had an "ah-ha" moment. I realized this is precisely the message I want to communicate. Life is a do-over! We have the chance to choose again. There is no law that decrees we have to remain in our original choices. We can learn how to make better selections that will get us to where we really want to be in life. If our present lives do not reflect our true selves — what is most important to us and what we love to do — things don't need to stay that way. We can ask for and receive a free second chance to design our life path.

I know firsthand about asking for a do-over in life. I left behind a stressful, demanding career as a trial attorney in California and created a more relaxed and fulfilling life as a life coach in southern Utah. What I'd like to do in this book is share my experience with you and the lessons I've learned along the way, and perhaps even motivate you to explore your own life do-over. It's a great journey that will lead you to a life of joy, ease, and fulfillment. All you have to do is ask....

A Life Do-Over Is a Second Chance to Design Your Path in Life

Simply stated, a life do-over is a chance to choose again in your life. It is an opportunity to make decisions and take actions based on what is completely right for you and will lead you in the direction you would really like to go. It is about making a conscious decision to look inside yourself, find out what matters most to you, and redesign your life to express the real you. Most of all it is about finding the path that will lead to your best life, the one you have dreamed about living.

Sometimes life's unexpected twists and turns force us into this reassessment process. This was certainly true for Phil in *City Slickers*. He was caught having sex with the cashier at the grocery store owned by his controlling father-in-law. This incident made him look long and hard at how unhappy he was with his life. Other situations that often trigger life do-overs include divorce, job termination, major illness, or loss of loved ones.

The good news is that we do not have to wait until life throws us such a severe curve ball. We can readjust our course in life and proactively make changes when we notice we are not in alignment with our true selves. This is what happened to me. I finally had enough of feeling unsatisfied and off course in my life, and I decided to explore new possibilities.

So, whether it is the result of a forced life change or a proactive decision to make life better, there are a lot of people out there exploring this idea of a life do-over. Here are a few life do-over situations that my coaching clients have shared with me:

• *A woman in her late thirties admits she is through with the stress of working full time as a critical care case manager and works instead as a traveling nurse, with lots of free time for biking and hiking*

• *A man in his mid-forties, laid off from a utilities company after working there for over twenty years, starts his own contracting business, which leaves more time to enjoy his family, his love of horses, and the outdoors*

• *A woman in her early forties leaves her career as a hairstylist, moves to Australia where her husband's family lives, and explores ways to reignite her passion for dance and choreography*

• *A woman in her late forties, forced into medical retirement, wants to better manage her physical limitations, reconnect with her love of crafts and jewelry, and find more joy in her life*

• *A man in his mid fifties leaves his unfulfilling job in sales to work with his wife as a campground host*

• *A woman in her mid forties, recovering from depression and exhaustion caused by caring for her disabled son, decides to learn how to take time for herself each week and write the book she has been thinking about for years*

• *A man in his thirties makes a decision to change jobs so he will not have to travel as much and can be home more to spend time with his young daughter*

• *A woman in her early fifties, laid off from a supposedly secure government job, takes a year off to travel before returning to work in a fun part-time job with a non-profit organization*

• *A woman attorney in her mid-forties decides to reduce her legal practice to part time so she can pursue becoming a certified fitness instructor and home decorator*

I am not the only one encountering people pursuing life do-overs. My coaching colleagues tell me that many of their clients are actively working on how to make new and different life choices. Moreover, Gail Sheehy acknowledges and documents this phenomenon in *New Passages: Mapping Your Life Across Time*, her sequel to the landmark bestseller *Passages*. Sheehy describes the process of exploring and asking for a do-over as the passage into second adulthood. "All of a sudden you have to start listening to the little voices inside: What do I really want to invest my life in? What do I really care about? How can I construct a life that fits the me of today as opposed to the me of 15 years ago? "

It is amazing to think about how many people may actually be going through a life do-over right now. The Baby Boomer generation, those born between 1946 and 1965, are right in the middle portion of their lives. Consider how many people each day are having the big birthdays—numbers 40 and 50—and taking an inventory of where they are in life. So, if you're going through this process of questioning the old and exploring the new, take comfort in knowing that you are definitely not alone.

I hope I've piqued your interest in this idea of a life do-over. It's a powerful, conscious decision you make to connect with your real self and make life choices that are totally right for you. It's about understanding that life is not a dress rehearsal, and there is no time like the present to redirect and redesign your life. It's about moving out of neutral and into action—positive forward motion toward the life you've dreamed about living. If you'd like to find out whether you are a candidate for a life do-over, take a few minutes to ponder the following questions.

Self-Assessment — Are You Ready for a Do-Over?

Consider the following statements and check those that are true for you.

❑ I've made it to the top of the ladder in my professional and/or personal life, but I'm no longer sure if the ladder is against the right wall.

❑ There are things that I love to do, which make me feel energized and alive, that I have not done in a long time.

❑ After the terrorist attacks of September 11, 2001, I vowed to spend more time with the people I love and remember my real priorities, but I have not followed this up with any concrete changes in my life.

❑ If I knew I only had a year to live, I could think of several things I definitely would have to do and experience before my time on Earth was over.

❑ If I knew I would succeed and did not have to worry about what other people would think of me, I would pursue a long-held dream.

❑ I want to explore the idea of a life do-over but don't know where I'd find the time or energy to add this to my already full plate.

❑ It is difficult to actually contemplate a life do-over because I don't know how to put my needs and wants at the top of my priority list.

❑ I think I know what changes I would like to make in my life, but I am stuck in neutral and afraid to move forward.

❑ My negative self-talk tells me I'm not good enough and don't deserve what I really want in life.

❏ I struggle with making life changes because I want to control the details and know precisely how they will turn out before I take action.

How many of these statements are true for you? If you are like most people who first take this assessment, there are probably several. Don't be alarmed. This is actually a positive sign. It means you are beginning to be honest with yourself about what is not working in your life, which is the first step toward making changes.

This is where I found myself several years ago. Many of these questions were true for me. As I found the nerve to admit this to myself, I took the first step in a life-altering process of designing a much better life. In fact, let me share my life do-over story with you.

My Life Do-Over Experience:
From Trial Attorney to Life Coach

My story begins when I was in my late thirties, living on the Central Coast of California. I was working as an attorney, first as a criminal prosecutor and then as an assistant city attorney. If you had observed me at that time, you would have described me as a happy and successful career woman. And in many ways, I was. I had a beautiful home on the California coast, a wonderful marriage, very talented and supportive people with whom I worked, and lots of friends and family. From the outside, things looked quite good.

The problem was that this life began to feel uncomfortable and unsatisfying. I remember a pivotal moment while walking on the beach, when I was overwhelmed with a sense of feeling trapped. I almost felt as if my breath was being choked out of me. As I looked down the road ten or twenty years, I knew that I could not keep practicing law. There had to be another way to earn a living that would allow me to more fully express my unique gifts and talents and live a relaxed and satisfying life.

I decided to keep a journal in order to talk to myself about these feelings. Little did I know at the time that I was actually finding a way to let my wise, inner voice speak to me. Until then

I had resisted the process of journaling, suffering from the "perfect writing" syndrome. I couldn't just write down random insights and impressions. Rather, I could only write down my thoughts if they were very wise insights, and I could come up with a solution for the problems my journaling identified. But now I made a pact with myself. This journal would be for my eyes only, and I would not create any rules about writing down my thoughts. I did not have to write every day. I only needed to write when I felt like it, and I would permit myself to write whatever felt like coming out in whatever format it chose.

With this new understanding, my journal became my confidant for my life do-over. Within its pages, I could admit some pretty scary things to myself: that I wanted more freedom and flexibility in my life; that I craved the experience of connecting with other people on a personal level about how their lives were or were not working for them; that I found the actual practice of law to be tedious, boring, and negative; and that I might be willing to trade in the security of a weekly paycheck to satisfy my growing desire for adventure and travel.

For almost a year I kept these thoughts pretty much to myself. I did, however, look for ways to make my law job more interesting and satisfying. I read many books about how to go through life transitions and make career changes. As I look back at that tumultuous year, I realize that I was building a foundation for the life-altering decisions I would soon be making.

My initial decision was to take a three-month leave of absence from my job to see if perhaps all I needed was a rest and a chance to recharge my battery. After all, I was a very driven young woman, being sworn in as a lawyer when I was just 25, and immediately beginning to work in the criminal trial courts of Los Angeles. I hoped that when I returned from my sabbatical I would feel refreshed and ready to recommit to my legal career.

When I resumed my job at the end of the leave of absence, I did feel more energized and focused for a few months. However, I soon found the feelings of discomfort and discontent resurfacing, and they felt even stronger after having had a taste of a different life.

In my journal, I confided how much I needed to make some permanent life changes. Here is a passage I wrote at the time, describing my discontent:

> *I feel very unfulfilled and stressed out at work when I see my life continuing on the same path. I want to work somewhere where my real talents of teaching, listening, and helping others are used, and where I feel fulfilled rather than drained at the end of the day. I firmly believe that my inner voice is crying out. I want to find a way to live and work with a greater sense of inner peace and personal fulfillment.*

A very pivotal event happened while I was looking at my options. Being 38 years old, I decided to have my first mammogram, especially since I was still on my employer's health insurance plan. I ended up needing to have a suspicious growth in my right breast biopsied. The entire process took over a month, and it provided me with plenty of time to consider all of the possibilities and experience a full range of emotions. In a very real way, I came face to face with my mortality. It made me ask whether I had any regrets about my life path and if I wanted to live differently for whatever time I had left.

On New Year's Eve, I received a call from my doctor with good news — the growth was benign. The silver lining of this experience was that I had to ask myself what I would do if the biopsy came back cancerous. I realized that after I received medical treatment, I would want to travel with my husband and find a way to teach and guide other people off the autopilot and into living consciously and authentically. Was I going to wait for a major life-threatening disease before I could give myself permission to do that? No! I realized that this could be my last year, and I wanted to seize the opportunity to do what felt right for me at this stage in my life.

Within a few days my husband and I decided to begin our life do-over. Although we did not know how the adventure would turn out, we were willing to take the chance. We created a plan for quitting our jobs, buying an RV, and traveling the country for one year.

We did not know what the outcome would be — whether we would come back to our home in California or what we would do for work. Because we did not want to make those decisions prematurely, we agreed to make no decisions while traveling, allowing ourselves to unwind and enjoy the adventure.

The yearlong trip was remarkable. It actually took me about four months to relax and get into the flow of each day. My original approach was to plan and organize our daily activities so that we saw and did everything possible. Fortunately, my husband continued to remind me that I was no longer on a schedule. I could let the days unfold at their own pace and settle into enjoying the moment. This was not a concept I was used to, but eventually I caught on.

I did continue to write in my journal and seek guidance from my inner voice about what new career I could pursue. By identifying the activities I really enjoyed doing and the aspects of my law career that I did like, I was able to begin describing my ideal life and job. It would involve travel and a flexible schedule, with me teaching and leading some type of personal development seminars and working with individuals to share the life lessons I was learning. I would often laugh and wonder how I could make a living doing that, but I tried not to worry about those details too often.

About nine months into the trip, I stopped at a bookstore in Dana Point, California, to have a cup of coffee and browse the bookshelves. I found myself drawn to a book, *Take Time for Your Life*, by Cheryl Richardson. Because I am often attracted to a book that turns out to be just what I need, I trusted this instinct and bought the book. It changed my life! The author described her own transition from financial planner to successful life coach. As she described the profession of life coaching, I was amazed to discover that it was exactly what I had been describing in my journal. By doing some research, I discovered several coach-training programs and how to connect with other people involved in the profession of life coaching.

Upon returning home, my husband and I decided to relocate to southern Utah, a place we were drawn back to several times during our trip. I was able to complete the two-year coach-training program through Coach U and make my dream career a reality. My husband also found a new line of work that he loves, and we have connected with some of the most wonderful people in our new home amidst the red rocks and desert of southern Utah.

Many people who hear my story tell me that I am courageous and brave, and they cannot imagine themselves taking such bold steps to turn their lives upside down. The funny thing is that I really don't see it as courage. I simply could not imagine myself continuing to live my old life for ten or twenty more years. My inner spirit was slowly dying, and fortunately, it had enough life left to cry out loudly and finally get my attention.

I am not suggesting that everyone needs to undertake such a drastic life do-over. What I do know is that once you begin the process of examining your life and asking yourself what you really want, very interesting and unexpected doors will begin to open. You will be presented with opportunities you hadn't even considered. The key is to be receptive to the possibilities and willing to take risks, large and small, in order to get in touch with your true self and live a really great life. Perhaps I should warn you to be careful what you wish for. But I know it is such a remarkable journey that you couldn't possibly regret your decision.

Why Doesn't Everyone Ask for a Life Do-Over?

At this point you are probably wondering if the idea of a life do-over is so great, why doesn't everyone ask for one? There are no reasons why they can't. There are, however, several excuses people use when faced with the opportunity to make new life choices. I had to struggle with each of these during my life do-over, and I'd like to review these briefly so you don't fall victim to them.

• *What would other people think of me*

Even if you are intrigued with what your life could look like if you made some new choices, you are probably also thinking about what other people would think of you if you did. I know this concern well. Can you imagine the reaction I got from people when I told them about my plans to leave my legal career and travel the country for a year with no idea of the ultimate outcome? That is probably why I waited for over a year to admit these feelings to my husband. Many people thought we were crazy, and worried that I was exiting a successful legal career at the most lucrative time. Fortunately, several close friends supported our decision and provided us with encouragement and support when we began to falter. I got to the point where I did not care whether others approved or understood, as I was listening to the beat of my own drummer, finally, and making decisions that felt right for me.

• *It seems awfully selfish to focus on my life*

I hear this a lot. People really struggle with putting themselves at the top of their priority list. It feels self-indulgent to focus on their own wants and needs, and they believe it is better to give most of their time and energy away to others. My answer is simple. It is not being selfish—it is being self-full. We are only good to others when we are also good to ourselves.

Have you ever wondered why the airplane safety instructions direct parents to put their own oxygen masks on *before* attending to their children's masks? That is because the parents would be of no use to their children if they did not first take care of getting oxygen to their own brain. This same idea holds true for each of us when we put everyone else's needs before our own. We aren't any good to others unless we are filling our own internal gas tank.

At a recent work/life balance seminar, I addressed this issue of feeling selfish when we learn to say no and set boundaries. A woman in the audience raised her hand and asked if she could share a story. She had been the kind of person who said yes to everyone's requests and always did what other people wanted her to do. Between her family and church commitments, she was exhausted and barely able to function. She finally snapped and spent several months in the hospital. Although she was well on her way to recovery and learning to take care of herself, she wanted the audience to know it is a matter of self-survival and good mental health to value your own wants and needs. I couldn't agree more.

• *I have plenty of time to get around to doing what I really want to do with my life*

This is just plain wrong. It is a byproduct of denying our own mortality. We don't like to think about the fact that our time is limited and the clock is ticking. Yet no matter how much we try to pretend otherwise, we do not necessarily have many years ahead of us. Besides, why should we wait for some future date to start really enjoying our lives and manifesting our heartfelt dreams and desires?

While on our RV trip, my husband and I talked with many people about why we had unplugged our careers in midstream and headed off in an RV at our relatively young ages. Over and over again, we heard stories about couples who had put off fun and adventure until retirement, only to have one partner become ill or die before they could enjoy their "golden years." There is simply no guarantee that we will have time down the road to do what we would really love to do.

How to Use This Book to Explore Your Own Life Do-Over

I debated long and hard about how to present my experiences and strategies so they would be the most interesting and useful to you, the reader. At one point I considered putting the exercises and action steps into a separate journal you could use when you were ready to begin exploring your life do-over. Then I thought about putting them into this book, perhaps in separate shaded boxes or at the end of each chapter. Because I wanted this book to appeal to people at all stages of the life do-over process, from simply being curious about the concept all the way to being in the midst of a life do-over, I knew there needed to be enough detail without seeming overwhelming.

When I asked friends and clients for their opinion, they gave me some interesting feedback. Several people admitted they do not feel comfortable writing in books, even when space is provided right in the text. Others shared that they feel guilty and a bit resentful if a book asks them to write down their thoughts yet they do not feel like doing it at that time. They explained that if they just want to browse through a book to see if the concepts make sense, the imposition of must-do exercises can be annoying. Still others indicated they liked the idea of having a designated area for capturing their personal reflections as they read the book so everything was in one place and easy to take along.

Given this input, I decided to have primarily text in the book and a small guided journal at the end as a place for you to record your thoughts and insights, if you are so inclined. You will find this journal at the back of the book as Appendix Two. Within the main portion of the book, I may pose a question for you to ponder or suggest specific tools or techniques for a particular life skill or strategy. I leave it up to you to decide what to do with the information. You can note it and file the data for possible future use. Alternatively, you can capture your ideas in the pages provided in the appendix. You can even get a separate journal, one that appeals to your eye and feels good in your hands. Only you can determine which process is right for you in exploring the new possibilities for your life.

If you decide to really dig in and undertake your own life do-over, I recommend reading through the entire book first to get the big picture. Let the concepts begin to sink in and start reflecting on your life. What is working and what isn't? What is missing? What gets you excited and makes your heart sing? Begin to put your focus and energy into what you would do if you could have a life do-over. Then go back through the specific strategies. You can either review them in order or start with the ones that speak the most strongly to you.

Consider this book and your journal pages to be a resource and safe place to have a dialogue with your wise, inner self. Take it with you. Get a favorite pen to use when writing down your thoughts. Be honest with yourself when doing this exploration. You don't have to take action immediately, but do take a realistic inventory of what changes you would like to see in your life. Give yourself permission, as I did, to break away from the need to have your writing be perfect. Limit the rules you place on yourself regarding your journal writing. Let it feel joyful, fun, and easy. You will be amazed by what you discover and the places this journey will take you!

> *Twenty years from now, you will be more disappointed by the things you didn't do than by the ones you did. So, throw off the bowlines. Sail away from the safe harbor. Catch the trade winds in your sails. Explore. Dream. Discover.*
>
> —Mark Twain

Strategy #1
Focus on Living from the Inside Out

What lies behind us and what lies before us
are tiny matters compared to what lies within us.

—Ralph Waldo Emerson

When we begin to feel restless in our lives and ready to explore new options, it is very tempting to look at what we can do differently. New jobs, locations, hobbies, and partners often seem to be the answer. While these changes may ultimately happen, they are not the place to start. Rather, we need to turn inward and reconnect with what is on the inside—with our true selves that have become buried over the years. This is the only way we can build a new life that really fits us and feels right.

This was certainly my experience. When I initially admitted that I wasn't satisfied with my life, the first impulse was to find a different legal job. I even explored the option of becoming a judge. In fact, several people approached me about submitting my name to the governor's judicial appointment committee. At first that sounded like a possible solution. However, once I got past the ego

15

stroking, I thought about what I would be doing each day. When I looked inside myself and measured this option against what was important to me—a flexible schedule, travel and adventure, and helping people create their best lives—I realized that pursuing a judgeship was in serious discord with what was important to me. Being tied to a rigorous court schedule and resolving arguments between attorneys all day long was not consistent with my true self.

However, I was a bit confused about how to get more in touch with my true self. As I turned inward and wrote how I was feeling in my journal, I discovered a wonderful source of wisdom. The answers to my questions did not come from acquiring or doing more, but from turning my attention inward. Getting to know myself—my values, passions, and gifts—opened the door for me, and continues to be my key life navigational tool. Three of the best ways to connect with the inside are:

> ➤ Start with who you want to be rather than what to do or what to have
> ➤ Know the true cost of your "stuff"
> ➤ Commit to some self-discovery time

Orient Yourself with the BE—DO—HAVE Model

One of my favorite ways to explain the idea of living from the inside out is with the BE—DO—HAVE model. To really understand this, let's start with the reverse, which is where our consumer-driven society is today.

HAVE	DO	BE
Have money	Do what impresses others	Be happy
Have possessions	Do what others expect	Be successful
Have power/respect	Do what feeds the ego	Be satisfied

Most people know at some level that this model does not work. Focusing on the "having" and "doing" as the way to be happy, successful, and satisfied with life comes up short every time. This reminds me of small children at Christmas. When they have several presents to open, they tear into each one, only pausing for a moment to see what is inside the box. The desire to keep opening new presents is definitely more important than enjoying what is inside the ones already unwrapped. The children seem insatiable, unable to focus on what they have received, and fixated exclusively on what is coming next. Of course, at some point, there are no more new gifts, and they do settle down and start playing with the toys. But for quite a while, their attention is on what is still to come rather than on what is right in front of them.

This is a good reminder of how we often seek the next big present under the tree. When we keep focusing on the "having" and the "doing," without first grounding our actions in "being," we will continue to feel like frenzied children at Christmas, never able to stop and just be in the moment and feel satisfied. It's not about getting what we want all the time, but rather wanting what we already have—an incredible mind, body, and spirit that contain all of the wisdom and guidance we will ever need in this lifetime.

That is why the model works so much better in the order of BE—DO—HAVE. Then we let our life choices be an extension of our "being," our true self that wants desperately to be heard and followed.

BE	DO	HAVE
Be authentic	Work that feeds mind & spirit	Life that feels right
Be fearless	What you feel like doing	Heartfelt desires
Be flexible	What shows up each day	Joy and ease

Actor Toby Maguire (*Spiderman, Seabiscuit*) understands this process of defining himself from his "being," and not from his "doing" or "having." During a recent interview, I heard him describe his reaction to being so successful at such an early age. He actually stopped acting at eighteen and spent months in a kind of philosophical retreat, questioning himself. Ultimately, he connected with his true inner being and realized that his work as an actor was not who he really was. It was only what he did.

I certainly understand what he was saying. I arrived at the same place when exploring the role my legal career played in my life. By getting a better handle on who I really was—my gifts, passions, and what was most important to me—I understood that I would still be that person whether I expressed it by doing legal work or by doing some other kind of work. Once we connect with our "being," the decisions about what to do and what to have are guided by truth and authenticity, which rarely lead us astray.

Know the True Cost of Your "Stuff"

When I first bring up this idea of living from the inside out, many people wonder if I am suggesting an austere lifestyle with few material comforts. Rest assured, I am not suggesting any such thing. I enjoy having lots of creature comforts. The trick is to know the true cost of our possessions, our "stuff," and not feel enslaved to the material things in our lives. If we are so beholden to debt and loans that we have no choices or flexibility in life, it makes any life changes very difficult.

It is actually quite simple to quantify the cost, in terms of your time and energy, of maintaining your stuff. List all the expenses associated with your stuff—home, cars, boats, motorcycles, RV—and figure out how much you have to pay each month to support that debt. Then, divide that by the number of hours you work each month. This will tell you how much debt you are working to pay for each hour that you work. It will also show you how much less you would need to work if you reduced some of your debt load.

This just might motivate you to look at ways to reduce your debt load. You can downsize your home, pay off loans for toys such as boats and RVs, find a way to bring in additional income, and/or follow a budget. And, of course, you could take a good look at whether you want to keep paying for all your stuff. Do you really want to work four hours each month just to pay for the boat that sits in the backyard for most of the year? Look at how much time you actually get to spend enjoying the item and how much it costs to keep it. Is it worth it? If not, consider how you can get out from under that debt.

This was quite an insight for me. As I was evaluating how to follow my real interests and passions, I remember realizing that I could choose how much stuff I really needed and wanted. If I pared down my stuff, I could live comfortably on less income and a whole lot less stress. The trade-off seemed to make a lot of sense. Ultimately, we bought a much smaller home and opted for a simpler life. This gave us the freedom to enjoy the moment without feeling obligated to a large debt load each month. You may come to a different resolution about how much stuff you want to support, but I urge you to at least look at this issue and decide if the hours required to maintain your material possessions are really worth it.

Commit to Self-Discovery Time

As you begin to switch your focus toward what is on the inside, you may feel a bit like a fish swimming upstream. My only advice is to expect resistance from others and accept that it will come. People tend to become defensive when we upset the apple cart by challenging the societal norm of "having" and "doing." The great thing is that the more you reorient yourself from the inside out, the more confident you will be in this process, and the less concerned you will be with the negative reactions of other people.

A great way to counter this resistance from others is to commit to some time to connect with and rediscover your true self. Try to spend some quality time each week turning inward, getting to know who you want to be in life, and listening to your wise, inner voice. This will take a commitment of time. While you are busy living *in* your life, it is crucial to take some time out so that you can work *on* your life. Most of us get so busy working in our lives that we have little time to work on our lives. You need to stop, take a break from the busy-ness of life, and take a strategic view of where you are going and what kind of a person you are being.

I offer two suggestions for creating this self-discovery time. First, make an actual date with yourself and keep it. Try blocking out an hour each week. Write it on your calendar or put it into your hand-held computer just as you would any other type of appointment. It is amazing how much we honor our commitments to other people, yet find countless ways to blow off the time we have set aside for self-care. We seem to value other people more than we do ourselves. To counter this, I strongly recommend making a solid date with yourself and viewing it as important as the other meetings and appointments you have during the week.

Second, find a special place where you can go by yourself and spend some quiet time. Try to block out as many distractions as you can. Select a place where you won't be interrupted. Turn your cell phone off, find a comfortable spot to sit, and provide your senses with as much positive input as possible. Beautiful music, lovely scenery, and tantalizing aromas can greatly enhance your self-discovery time.

I've had several special places. My mind and body seem to know to shift gears when I enter them. I look for locations that have very positive and uplifting energy, which I absorb when I am there. While working in San Luis Obispo, I discovered the secluded rear garden at the Downtown Mission. With a roomy wooden bench and a view of roses, trees, and foothills, this spot became my special place to visit during my lunch break.

Since moving to southern Utah, I've discovered a new special place — the spacious green lawn under the tree canopy in front of the lodge at Zion National Park. Because it is only thirty minutes from my house, I can retreat to this spot often. In fact, I went there many times while I was writing this book. I've also found coffeehouses to be a great place to get lost in my own thoughts. I'm sure there is a beautiful and nurturing place nearby that you can claim for your own special place, where you can open up and get reacquainted with what's on the inside.

During this process of reorienting from the inside out, expect to feel a bit restless and uncomfortable at first. That is okay. Stay with it. Use your journal to record these thoughts and questions. Keep setting some time aside and work through the resistance. You have probably not listened to and honored your true self in a long time, and it will take a while to reconnect. Rest assured that this commitment of your time and energy will pay very big dividends.

First say to yourself what you would be;
and then do what you have to do.

—Epictetus, Greek philosopher

Strategy #2
Connect with the Real You

Jackson Jackson was a good kid
He had four years of college and a bachelor's degree
Started workin' when he was 21
Got fed up and quit when he was 43
He said, "My whole life I've done what I'm supposed to do
Now I'd like to maybe do something for myself
And just soon as I figure out what that is
You can bet your life I'm gonna give it hell."

> — *The Real Life*
> by John Cougar Mellencamp

If you decide to reorient your decisions and actions from the inside out and spend some quality time working on your life, what can you expect to uncover? The "real you" — your true north, your internal reference point for selecting from the myriad of possibilities presented during your lifetime. This real you is made up of three key elements: your priorities, passions, and gifts. And, to make things even more interesting, your life's purpose is to get to know the real you, honor your priorities, and live fully from your passions and your gifts.

I've learned a lot about connecting with my real self. When I listen to and follow my real self, life seems easier and more satisfying. Conversely, when my choices and actions are not in alignment with my authentic self, I can feel the disconnection. I experience anxiety, doubt, and frustration. Life feels challenging and difficult.

I recall a good example of this feeling of disconnection when I was still practicing law but getting close to admitting I wanted out. I was at a settlement conference with several obnoxious attorneys arguing about a construction defect lawsuit. For a moment, all I heard was "blah, blah, blah," and I observed myself from outside of my body. I felt trapped and very sad. In that moment, I heard my true self crying out, reminding me that I could choose another profession and lifestyle. I did not have to continue practicing law! I remember smiling to myself and receiving a strange look from one of the opposing attorneys. I knew then that I had opened a crack of truth about my real self and it felt as though fresh air was flowing back into my life.

As I began writing in my journal and asking what I really wanted for my life, I discovered that I had forgotten who I really was. Getting so caught up in the "doing" and "having," I had lost sight of who I was *being*, or not being. This inquiry led me to answer three simple but profound questions, which I invite you to contemplate:

➢ What is important to you
➢ What do you love to do
➢ What are you meant to do

Answering these three questions may be more challenging than you think, but keep asking them. When you can confidently and effortlessly answer them, you will be well on your way to reconnecting with the real you. When you start to realize who you are at the authentic level of your being, then you will be able to make new life choices that are absolutely right for you.

What Is Important to You

This sounds like a simple question. It should be easy to say how you want to spend your time—the people you want to focus on, the activities you want to do, and the lifestyle you want to live. Yet I find many people struggle with this question. If this sounds like you, I've got several ideas to help you connect with the values and priorities that are most important to you.

To begin with, we need to be clear about the definition of the term "values and priorities." These are *personal* values and priorities. I am not talking about social norms or moral codes of conduct. That is a different discussion. Personal values and priorities encompass the people, lifestyle, personal code of conduct, and activities that matter to you. They are the interactions and behaviors that feel right to you and bring you a sense of well-being. They are what you know for sure to be true for you, deep in the core of your being. When you are honoring your values and priorities, you feel most like yourself, and you greet each day fully present, alive, and engaged.

A simple way to connect with your values and priorities is to think back to what you did in the hours and days immediately following the terrorist attacks on the World Trade Center and the Pentagon. Who did you feel compelled to call? With whom did you spend your time? What thoughts did you have about what is most important to you?

I remember hearing and reading about the profound life changes people made in the days and months after that horrific event. People who had been in those buildings and escaped often made life-altering decisions, some to pursue new careers with non-profit agencies, others to join the Peace Corps, and still others to move back to their hometowns and take over family businesses. That kind of cataclysmic occurrence acts like a powerful magnifying glass to our real selves. It seems to strip away what is not important.

During my life do-over, I learned several things about identifying what is important, and I'd like to share those insights with you.

- *Values and priorities are unique to each one of us*

Although family and society can expose us to various options, ultimately we must decide what is right for us. And this may be very different from our parents' values or the accepted norms. When we set about to discover our real selves, we need to be prepared to embrace what is true for us, even if it means admitting we are attracted to the road less traveled. This involves separating what others think we should do from what we really want to do and choosing how to spend our time.

- *Values and priorities are created equal*

There is no scale for rating or judging one person's values against another's. I may not agree with or understand what is important for you, but that does not diminish your choice. This concept is woven throughout the United States Constitution, proclaiming that each person is entitled to life, liberty, and the pursuit of happiness. Of course, there are common sense limitations on what can be called a value or priority. Causing physical or emotional harm to another cannot be allowed in an orderly society, and I am assuming we all agree with this premise.

- *We can use our values and priorities as our life compass*

Knowing what is important to us grounds us to the inside-out perspective, allowing us to stay on a true course on the new life paths we choose for ourselves. This idea is echoed in the words of Richard Bellamy in *12 Secrets for Manifesting Your Vision, Inspiration, and Purpose*: "Unless we have an object of intangible value as our focus of attention ... we are like a ship of mutinous fools who have thrown the captain and navigator overboard. We are cursed to be pushed by the wind and pulled by the currents on a chaotic and uncertain journey."

I know the feeling of being on a chaotic and uncertain journey. That is where I found myself a few years ago. It was quite startling to realize that although I was "successful," my life did not reflect what was important to me and how I really wanted to live. I began noticing how much I valued flexibility with my work and home time, reading personal growth books, sharing life strategies with others, and free space in my life for travel and adventure to quench my "gypsy spirit." Yet, my life did not reflect those values. I was in a job that had tight control on my time, immersed me in an environment of problem solving and crisis intervention, and left me feeling drained at the end of the day.

Feeling petrified that my life would continue like this forever, I vowed to start acknowledging what was important to me and making life choices that were better aligned with what I wanted for my life. By using my journal to own up to what was most important to me, I connected with the people, activities, and lifestyle that I wanted to have in my life and the personal rules of conduct by which I wanted to start living. I encourage you to spend some time doing this important personal exploration and see what you uncover.

What Do You Love to Do

The answer to this question will be a special subset of your values and priorities, often referred to as talents, interests, or passions. These activities make our hearts sing and feed our souls. They connect us with the highest and best part of ourselves, making us feel immensely happy and deeply satisfied.

The list of what people love to do is incredibly long and varied. Fly fishing, golfing, drawing, writing short stories, hiking, running marathons, NASCAR racing, playing the guitar, river rafting, and gourmet cooking are some of the interests and passions pursued by my family members and friends. There truly is an endless variety of things that people love to do.

I have always loved reading personal growth/metaphysical books and sharing what I learn with others. This accounts for my attraction to political theory and philosophy courses in college. I can spend hours reading a new book and taking notes. It is how I relax and enjoy myself. When I was in the middle of changing my life course, I set a goal to find some type of new work that would allow me to pursue this passion. What a joy it was to discover the profession of life coaching and begin a new career that would allow me to do what I love to do!

When I speak about pursuing our passions, a frequently asked question is whether focusing on our desires isn't somehow decadent. I understand that many religions teach that we need to suppress our desires because they are ego-driven and selfish. This is especially true in America with our Puritan heritage. I respond to these concerns with a simple answer. Your passions and desires were placed in your heart by design and it is the suppression of these natural desires that creates problems. When we honor and pursue our talents and passions, keeping in mind the highest and best good for everyone around us, we are expressing our authentic selves. And that is a very good thing.

I have found three tools to be particularly useful in helping people connect with their passions and desires. Read through them and see which ones work for you.

• *Notice how you feel when you are engaged in activities*

Look for a sense of inner fulfillment — being in a state of ease and comfort, feeling energized and refreshed, and finding time has flown by while you were totally engaged in that activity. Become more aware of what you daydream about doing, longing for the time when you can get back to that activity.

• *Pay attention to the clues that surround you each day*

⌗ Books – Take a moment and look through your collection of books. Do you notice any common subjects or themes? Which books are your all-time favorites? Why?

⌗ News – Are there certain sections of the paper that you turn to first, or certain magazines that you love to read?

⌗ Movies – What movies have inspired you? Are there certain movies that you watch over and over again? Why? Once again, look for common themes.

⌗ People – Who are the inspirational people in your life? Who do you admire? Whose example do you strive to follow? Is there someone you can think of right now who inspires your passion?

• *Ask yourself three powerful questions*

⌗ What would you do if you absolutely, positively knew you would succeed?

⌗ What would you do if you didn't have to worry about what others would think of your actions?

⌗ What would you do if you knew you only had a year to live?

I had a chance to focus on this last question while going through the breast biopsy process. I was often tempted to give up my plans and pull the plug on my life do-over. Whenever I doubted my new path, I would remember how lucky I was to have the opportunity to reconnect with my real self and make new life choices. The inspiring words of Ralph Waldo Emerson became my mantra, which I still try to follow every day: "I will do strongly before the sun and moon whatever inly rejoices me and the heart appoints."

What Are You Meant to Do

Most people are quite perplexed by this question. It is often presented as finding your life purpose or creating a personal mission statement — concepts which are difficult for many people to grasp. I have discovered a much easier way to answer this question. You are meant to share your gifts with the world, and your gifts are what you have been doing for other people your whole life. So, if you want to do what you are meant to do, you need to identify and share your special gifts with the world. It is really that simple.

I have to give a big thanks to a very generous friend and colleague, Jane Miner, for getting me excited about this concept of individual gifts. At one of our first meetings, Jane asked me what I thought my gifts might be. At first, I said they must be speaking, writing, and connecting with people. But as Jane pointed out, those were actually *skills*. My *gifts* were deeper. Jane shared that one of her gifts was to be an "idea distiller." She loves to read and ponder gems from life strategy books and distill them into succinct, learnable concepts. As Jane explained, we can't help but express our gifts, as they naturally flow from us and are an integral part of who we really are.

After this conversation, I began to take a closer look at my gifts and have some fun finding just the right words to describe them. Later in this section, I will share more of what I've discovered about my unique gifts. But first, I'd like to explore why recognizing our gifts and living from them is such an important part of a life do-over.

It is amazing how most people who decide to make some life changes focus on what is missing in their lives and what needs to be improved. Little attention is given to what they are doing well and the gifts they have to offer. How much time, if any, do you spend focusing on your gifts? It is definitely time to get started on your own gift quest.

What is so interesting about our gifts is that when we are sharing and using them, we actually end up replenishing our own life force. In honoring and expressing our gifts, we add fuel and nourishment to our inner power source. I am not the only one who has noticed this positive return. Alexandra Stoddard, in her beautiful book, *Choosing Happiness*, reminds us of what we gain when we share our gifts: "When we spend our lives using our gifts, we are playing our part in the human drama...and we gain a vibrancy, a love of life, to share with others."

In addition to recharging our batteries, honoring and sharing our gifts makes our work and play a lot more fun—almost magical. A powerful example of how wonderful life becomes when we use our gifts is the way Oprah Winfrey's career has exploded since she got very clear about her gift for using the media (television and magazines) as a catalyst for positive change in people's lives. She often speaks about her moments of clarity as to what she is here to do and how her gifts and talents are to be used. Her fame, wealth, and status have soared, but I get the distinct impression these are not her main motivators. Rather, Oprah seems to want to do the work she was put on Earth to do, and she knows that the rest will follow.

I hope by now you are ready to explore your own special gifts. I found it to be a fun and exciting process, but I did not uncover them overnight. It took some time, as well as a willingness to share my ideas with others in order to get their perspective and insights. Here are a few ideas to get you started on your gift discovery.

• *Look at your life—what themes do you notice?*

For example, I realized that I have always been involved with creating organizations and communities. From Girl Scouts to community theater to women's golf groups, I could see a definite pattern throughout my life.

- *What can you not help yourself from doing and what do you just do because it feels so natural and easy?*

As my friends and family will attest, I have always loved to share the personal growth concepts from the books I read, especially if I think they could be useful to someone on their path in life. I just can't help myself.

- *What do people say you do for them*

Although you may not recognize what you do naturally as a gift, other people will see your gifts much more clearly. Choose a few friends and family members and ask for their input about what you do for other people. I received consistent feedback about being a great listener and motivator. I was also told that people always had a clearer idea of how to go forward in life after talking to me.

- *Start with your skills and talents, and then find the unique gifts underneath*

After first identifying my skills as speaking, writing, and connecting with people, I soon realized that I had been given these tools in order to share my special gifts with the world.

- *Find the right language to accurately describe your particular gifts*

You may want to use the noun-verb combination. I found this to be very helpful, and I have come to identify my core gifts as:

- ⌺ People Developer
- ⌺ Idea Sharer
- ⌺ Community Creator

I now focus on finding ways to use my gifts in my work and in my play. That is why I design my workshops and retreats with an eye toward creating a sense of closeness and community among the participants. Since I can't stop myself from being a community creator, I might as well go with it and consciously tap into this gift. And since I have tapped into it, my workshops and retreats have been much more successful and enjoyable for everyone.

Here are some additional examples that clients and workshop participants have shared with me when they have used the above suggestions to identify their unique gifts:

- ♯ Adventure Seeker
- ♯ Community Healer
- ♯ Diamond Shiner
- ♯ Energy Infuser
- ♯ Fun Instigator
- ♯ People Beautifier
- ♯ Puzzle Solver
- ♯ Rare Treat Finder
- ♯ Storyteller
- ♯ Voice Encourager

The main thing is to have fun with the process of identifying your gifts. Once you begin the gift quest, you won't be able to stop. You'll realize, as I did, that you want to find more and more ways to incorporate your gifts into both your work life and your leisure time, because it just feels so right for you. Good! This is a clear indication that you are connecting with and honoring the real you.

I love Wayne Dyer's admonition not to die with your music still in you. I would actually take it one step farther and encourage you not to die without getting to know the real you—your priorities, passions, and gifts. Because until you do, you will continue to drift through life without a clear sense of direction, missing opportunities to have what you really want and live the life you are meant to live.

Be yourself; no base imitator of another, but your best self. There is something which you can do better than another. Listen to that inward voice and bravely obey that. Do the things at which you are great, not what you were never made for.

—Ralph Waldo Emerson

32

Strategy #3
Make Life Choices Consistent with the Real You

The trouble with so many of us is that we underestimate the power of simplicity. We have a tendency to overcomplicate our lives and forget what's important and what's not.··· And as the pace of life continues to race along in the outside world, we forget that we have the power to control our lives regardless of what's going on outside.

—Robert Stuberg

Once you have reconnected with the real you, it may seem like you are miles away from that personality. You are probably wondering how you got so far off course. The simple answer is that it's the life choices—the seemingly small and insignificant ones all the way to the big earth-shattering ones—that have taken you away from the person you really want to be and the life you are meant to live. When you make choices without consulting with and receiving guidance from the real you, it is no surprise that you arrive at a strange place.

I often think about the impact small mistakes make while navigating at sea. When a set direction is a few degrees off course, the vessel will arrive at a very different location than originally intended after several hours of traveling. Is it any wonder we find ourselves sailing for very strange and unintended shores when we allow ourselves to drift aimlessly without consulting our internal compass?

The key to getting where you want to go in life is to consciously and deliberately keep your priorities, passions, and gifts front and center and frequently ask whether your pending life choices will take you closer to or farther away from them. To help you with this, I have developed a three-step process you can use to make life choices that are in alignment with your real self:

> ➢ Create your own YES List from the self-discoveries you made in the last chapter
> ➢ Consult your YES List often, especially when faced with a request for your time and energy or a new option to pursue
> ➢ If you decide a particular request or option is not aligned with your YES List, say NO to that opportunity

Learning to say both YES and NO with confidence and without feeling guilty are critical life skills that you can learn. Until you do, you will experience the constant frustration of feeling as though you are living a life you did not choose and wasting valuable time that could be spent doing what you'd love to be doing. You will feel trapped in a life not of your choosing. Let me help spring you from this trap by taking a detailed look at each one of these steps.

Create Your YES List

In the last chapter, we discussed how to connect with the real you, which includes your priorities, passions, and gifts. Hopefully you have a better understanding of what is truly important to you, what makes your heart sing, and what you have to share with others. This is the foundation for creating your YES List. What five things are the key to who you really want to be right now, in this moment in life? How do you most want to spend your time? What people are truly important to you? Which activities would make you feel the most complete? The answers to these questions make up your YES List.

Resist the temptation to identify more than five items. If you overload yourself, you run the risk of feeling so overwhelmed that you will not be able to focus on anything. Over time, you can modify your list. As you get to know yourself better and become even clearer on what you need to do to live your best life, your YES List will change. The key is to focus on five items at a time.

When I have given this assignment to clients, I frequently find they are a bit reluctant to complete the task. They think the items they place on their YES List must be extremely significant, lofty, big-ticket items. Spending time walking their dog, cooking and eating an evening meal with their family, playing the guitar, or enjoying the evening newspaper just don't seem momentous enough to write down on a YES List, even though those are the kinds of things that are very important to their happiness and well-being.

If this sounds like what you are thinking, I'd like to help you switch out of this mindset. No one will judge your priorities. This is not a contest. It is simply a way to bring into focus, for this time in your life, the essential people and activities you need for a happy and meaningful life. And, you can rewrite your YES List as often as you like. You'll find that what is important to you at one stage in your life is not that important later. For example, when you are single, you may want lots of social interaction and a big circle of friends, whereas when you are married with a young family, those priorities will change. Let go of the need to create a "perfect" YES List for the ages. Instead, just tap into your heart and feelings and recognize what you want and need to have in your life at this moment in time.

Once you create your YES List, I strongly suggest that you write it down. When we keep thoughts and ideas in our heads, they tend to be forgotten. The act of putting pen to paper has amazing power. Not only do we remember the items that are written down, but they become much more real to us. It is as if we transfer them from the realm of possibility to reality. This is especially true if we post our YES List in several places so we can see it frequently. I like to post mine on my computer, the bathroom mirror, and even my steering wheel. By finding places that I naturally look at throughout the day, I feed my mind and spirit with what I really want to have in my life. It keeps me motivated and focused.

Putting together your YES List can actually be a very fun project. Rather than just writing down a few words, you can use pictures, photos, or any visual reminder of what you most want to be, do, and have in your life. I can still remember how much I enjoyed having pictures of our RV on my desk at work in the months leading up to my life do-over. I even included a small map of the United States and the places we intended to visit in our RV. Having the images right in front of me provided strength and clarity whenever I became doubtful or confused about what I was planning.

If you want to significantly increase the power of your YES List, try sharing it with other people. Just as writing it down adds power to your list, speaking what you want takes it to the next level. When you hear yourself tell others what is most important to you, you start to believe it. Moving from thought to word tells your wise, inner self that you are committed and ready to receive.

Use Your YES List to Evaluate Life Choices

If you did nothing else but create your YES List, you would benefit from this exercise by bringing what you want to have in life to the forefront of your thinking. But you need not stop there. The real value in creating your YES List lies in using it to decide how you do, and do not, want to spend your time. One of the most exciting and exasperating things about life is that we are presented with a variety of choices and opportunities each day. Our inherent free will allows us to select from a vast array of possibilities. The problem is that most people have no system for helping them make life choices. Instead, they either randomly select or allow other people to make decisions for them. Then they complain about not having the life they want.

A more effective strategy for making life choices, and the one that will greatly assist you in your life do-over, is to compare a new opportunity against your YES List. Does this option align with what you want to be, do, and have in your life? It may appear to be a really exciting possibility, as the judgeship did for me, but if it is not in synch with your YES List, it will lead you down a path that doesn't fit the real you.

Of course, this means you need to give yourself some time before you jump into something new or agree to undertake an additional activity. Most of us say yes for all the wrong reasons. We feel guilty if we say no, and obligated to say yes because we don't want to let other people down. We are more concerned with what others will think of us than we are with protecting our own YES List. The next time you are faced with a request for your time, even if it sounds very attractive, resist the temptation to give an immediate answer. Explain that you will need some time to consider it, and then do so. Look at your YES List and see whether the request aligns with your values and priorities, and whether it is something connected to your passions and interests. If the answer to either of these questions is no, why are you considering saying yes?

We can't blame other people for asking us to become involved or undertake a project. Others are just as busy as we are, and it is only natural for them to look for a way to offload some things from their own overburdened plates. And frankly, our YES List is not that important to them. It is our responsibility to guard our YES List by taking some time before we respond to new options and deciding if saying yes is the best choice for us.

Learn to Say NO

If in fact, the option presenting itself is not consistent with our YES List, it is essential that we are able to say "no" without feeling guilt and anxiety. I truly believe it is much easier to say no when we understand that doing so is a way of consciously saying yes to that which is most important to us. When we know what we do want in our lives, we realize that we cannot possibly have that while saying yes to every request for our time and attention. However, knowing this on a rational level does not mean that saying no will be easy.

There are many reasons why we struggle with saying no. One of the most common challenges is the tendency to worry about disappointing people when they ask for our assistance. I find this very interesting—we are more concerned with other people's feelings than we are with our own priorities and passions. This invariably leads to resentment and unhappiness, which means that we aren't even doing what others request of us with any dedication. So, although we tried to make them happy by saying yes, we may actually end up disappointing them because our heart was not in the task. I have found it is much better to be more selective about saying yes, and then give our full attention to the activity because we *want* to be involved.

Another common obstacle to saying no is we feel it is our duty to help, especially with community activities. If we don't do it, who will? My answer to that is there are often people who would like to get involved, but they are not asked. Instead, the same few people retain the power and then relish their roles as the martyrs of the organization. One of my clients shared that she secretly wanted to be the chairperson of a particular event but did not have the courage to step up and ask for it. When several people declined the position, it was offered to her, and she was very pleased to accept. Sometimes when we say no we are making room for others to have the opportunity to say yes.

After participating in many organizations, I have come to realize that if no one wants to get involved, maybe it's time to look at whether the organization has outlived its usefulness. There are times when it is okay to admit the purpose of an event or association has been met or is no longer compelling. I have noticed this to be the case with many of the women's organizations that were begun in the 1970s during the feminist movement. With membership declining, many of these groups are asking if there is still a need to band together to promote equal rights and opportunities for women. Perhaps the majority of our society has accepted the concept and the goals of these women's advocacy groups have been met. It is certainly appropriate to look at whether there is a continuing need for and interest in the organization's mission.

Probably the biggest reason people don't say no when they would like to is because they don't know how. Think about it. We certainly are not taught this in school, and family dynamics undermine many of our early efforts to honestly say yes and no. The good news is that saying no with clarity and conviction is a skill that can be learned, practiced, and mastered. The following are a few tips you can use to develop your NO muscle.

- *Remember, "No" is a complete sentence*

You don't have to go into lengthy explanations about why you are saying no. Politely decline, and if you must, state that you don't have time or it doesn't fit into your life right now.

- *Role-play saying no with a trusted friend*

This is especially helpful if you are facing a particularly difficult person or situation. Getting more comfortable with having the words come out of your mouth will make saying no much easier.

- *Remind yourself that by saying no, you are actually saying yes to what is most important*

You must keep your priorities in mind if you want to see your YES List come to fruition.

- *You can leave the door open to saying yes in the future*

Let the requestor know that your priorities and time commitments may change in the future, and you might reconsider at a later date.

One thing I know for sure is that human beings enjoy gathering together for common purposes and functions. I don't worry that if given the chance to say no, people will never say yes again. We all have our particular interests, and we will get involved when it makes sense for us. Wouldn't it be great if we served on boards and participated in groups because we wanted to and found that such service aligned with our YES List? Think of the energy and enthusiasm that would be generated!

These suggestions will give you a jumpstart on how to make life choices that are consistent with your YES List and represent what you truly want to do. While it is tempting to blame everyone and everything else for our inability to have time for ourselves, this is misplaced anger. The fault lies squarely on our own shoulders. The silver lining is that you can turn things around and insist that nothing get in the way of your priorities and passions. By creating a YES List, taking time to decide if a new option aligns with that list, and calling on your firm, strong NO muscle if needed, you can redesign your path in life and arrive at the destination of your choosing.

> *Saying yes and no clearly builds confidence and*
> *rids us of the misconception that we are powerless.*

—Marsha Sinetar

Strategy #4
Create Room for YOU in Your Life

What I know for sure is that how you spend your time defines who you are. I try not to waste time—because I don't want to waste myself. I'm working on not letting people with dark energy consume any of my time. I've learned that the hard way, after giving up hours of myself and my time, which are synonymous when you think about it.

—Oprah Winfrey

At this point I am going to assume you have begun to connect with the real you and are interested in making life choices consistent with the real you. Yet, as excited as you may be about taking advantage of your life do-over, chances are you often find yourself drained and exhausted at the end of the day, wondering how you will find the time or energy for *you* in your life. As good as a new and better life sounds, you doubt whether you can make it happen.

Trust me. I hear this over and over again. The average person is so busy with just getting through the day, it seems like an impossible task to get off the merry-go-round and focus on making a life change. This sense of inertia is why so many people stay stuck in lives that do not serve them well. What I propose is to start creating a reserve of time and energy that you can draw on for your life

41

do-over. To help with this challenging process of carving out space for you in your life, I offer the following suggestions for you to try:

> Create more free time by keeping a Time Chart for a week and finding out exactly where your time is going and whether you truly want to spend it that way

> Generate more energy by getting rid of the energy vampires who are sucking the lifeblood out of you and the physical and emotional clutter that is draining your life force

> Remember to fill up your internal gas tank often and take very good care of yourself

Before I review these techniques, I'd like to spend a few moments on two important concepts. First, this is not really about time management. That is a misnomer. There isn't any way to "manage" time. We all get twenty-four hours a day, and those hours pass at the same rate for each of us. What we *can* do is learn how to manage ourselves—how we choose to spend our time and where we allow our energy to go. It is all about self-management. The good news is that we can develop better self-management skills and become mindful of where we are squandering our time and energy.

Second, as you have probably already noticed, when I talk about creating room for you in your life, this involves more free time as well as additional energy. It won't do you any good to have a few extra hours each week if you are exhausted and drained when you crawl into bed, barely maintaining your sanity. It is really two sides of the same coin. When you create the free time, this energizes you and as you develop more energy, you can focus on where you are wasting your time. Both are critical life skills you must master if you are going to have room for *you* in your life.

Create More Free Time

The crucial first step in creating more free time is to find out where your time is currently going. If you wanted to get your finances in order, the first step would be to keep track of how you are spending your money during a particular week or month. This is the same analysis for your time. Do you really know how you are spending your twenty-four hours each day? Most of us have a general idea, but that is not sufficient. You need to analyze each hour and the choices and time allocations you make every day. The best way to do this is to create a time chart and write down, in hour segments, where your time really goes for one week. Try to record your activities at least twice a day so that you can get an accurate assessment.

As you record your time expenditures, you'll want to pay particular attention to the activities you find hard to admit to and the amount of time you are spending on them. In order to create an accurate picture of where you are choosing to spend time, you need to be honest and write these down. No one else has to look at your time chart. You can and should tuck it away each day in a private place. However, recognize the guidance you are receiving from your wise, inner voice in the form of guilt pangs. These are valuable clues about the time drains you can eliminate.

Set aside an hour at the end of the week to analyze your time chart. Now, I realize this may be a conundrum. You are doing this exercise because you do not have enough time, and I am asking you to set aside time for this. May I once again remind you to schedule a one-hour appointment with yourself? Put it on the calendar, just as you would a business or doctor's appointment, and keep it. Treat yourself to the same respect you would give to someone else who wanted an hour of your time. I daresay you are just as important.

When you analyze your Time Chart, look at the following questions and see which ones are most helpful in identifying your time drains.

• *Consider these questions about a particular activity to find out where you may be squandering your time:*

◻ Does this activity align with my YES List?
◻ Does this activity enhance my health or happiness?
◻ Does this activity really have to be done now or ever?

• *Look at how much of your time is spent caring for others*

This includes time that is committed to your children, parents, spouse, and friends. Spending time on and with these people is very important for a healthy and balanced life, but it is equally important to spend time doing activities that nurture your own mind, body, and spirit. How much time did you spend on self-care this week?

• *Could you delegate and/or offload some activities*

Have you thought about finding someone else to clean the car, run your errands, organize your office, or handle your bookkeeping? Given how busy our lives are these days, delegating tasks is an important way to make time for yourself and the activities that you enjoy. If you aren't sure what activities you could delegate, try this exercise:

⊠ For a week, keep a pad of paper handy and jot down every task that you don't enjoy doing and that someone else could do.

⊠ At the end of the week, brainstorm who could do those tasks for you, perhaps for a small fee.

⊠ Break the delusion of total self-reliance. Other people can and will do a good job to help out, if you will only give them a chance.

⊠ Be open to other people's ways of getting tasks done. Resist the need to micro-manage when you do delegate to someone else. Keep an open mind.

Once you have identified your time drains and the obstacles that are preventing you from reaching out to others for help, decide what changes you want to make with regard to how you spend your time. You may discover that you need to review the ideas previously discussed in Strategy #3 about saying no to the requests other people make on your time. That is fine. Take the time to reread that section and further develop your NO muscle. I know that doing this time chart exercise will prove to be very helpful in rooting out hidden time drains and creating more room in your life for what is most important to you.

Generate More Energy

Equally as important as creating more free time is having sufficient energy to take advantage of that additional time. This will involve examining two sources of energy drains—the people in your life who are energy vampires, and the unresolved piles of emotional and physical clutter you trip over throughout the day. Imagine what life would be like if you could focus on your YES List items without being sidetracked by the negative influences of certain co-workers, friends, and family members, and without unfinished projects and unproductive situations filling your thoughts and distracting you from what is really important.

This is actually easier than you think. Once you identify the energy drains, there are specific tactics you can use to reduce, if not eliminate them. Then you can watch for new ones entering into your life, and deal with them before they burrow in and start depleting your lifeblood.

- *Deal with the energy vampires in your life*

Take a few minutes to inventory the people in your life. Include family members, friends, co-workers, and social acquaintances. How do you feel when you are with them? Do you look forward to spending time together? Or do you dread those conversations and visits? Do your exchanges feel even, with give and take, or is the focus always on the other person? By now, you probably have a few people in mind who are your energy vampires. Perhaps you recognize these specific types:

⌑ Ms. Not My Fault

She consistently sees herself as a victim in life and blames others for her problems. Everything and everyone else create havoc for her. She takes no personal responsibility for what has become of her life.

⌑ Mr. Moan and Groan

He complains about what isn't working in his life, but never does anything about it. He asks you for advice, yet does not intend to use any of your suggestions.

¤ Ms. Self-Absorbed

She focuses all conversations around herself and expects you to be interested in all of the details of her life without ever asking about what is happening with you. She is summarized by this line from Bette Midler—"Enough about me, let's talk about you. What do you think of me?"

¤ Mr. Big I Am

He always has a story to one-up what you are talking about. He has done it all and seen it all. He loves to hear the sound of his own voice and never considers that you may have something of value to add. You wind up just listening and give up trying to have a dialogue.

¤ Ms. Gossip

She can't wait to tell you the latest scoop about how someone else is having trouble in life. She betrays the confidences of others and makes herself feel better by pointing out everyone else's failures. You know she will tell the next person everything you share with her.

¤ Mr. Take, Take, Take

He does not understand that relationships are a two-way street and expects you to meet all of his requests without reciprocating. He leaves you feeling dumped on and unappreciated.

Do any of these energy vampires sound familiar? I bet you have a heavy, uncomfortable feeling when you think about dealing with them. Consider how much wasted time and energy you spend on these people. What if you could find a way to shield yourself from their negative impact? Well, you can!

The most obvious way is to eliminate them from your life. This strategy works well with friends and acquaintances you have elected to bring into your life. There is nothing wrong with deciding that the negative energy far outweighs the positive aspects of a friendship. It's okay if you no longer want to have that person in your life. Yet most people balk when I make this suggestion. We get so caught up with not wanting to hurt someone's feelings or worrying about what they will think of us, that we are willing to sacrifice our own happiness rather than be forthright and end the relationship.

Because it can be so difficult to tell someone directly that you no longer want to spend time together, there are other steps you can take to put space between yourself and another person. Stop making dates to see them, explaining that you need some time for self-care, which is always true. Limit the amount of time you are available for their phone calls by screening your calls. Tell them that you are focusing on your passions and pursuits and don't have as much time for other people right now.

I have found that most of these energy vampires will seek out new people to whom they can attach themselves. Remember, you are really not that important to them. What *is* important to them is to have an energy donor. They will find someone else to fill your role if you are not available.

If they do ask why you are pulling away, you need to be honest about your desire to break free. Find a way to be as gentle as possible, but be honest. Explaining that your life is taking a different path and you are no longer going in similar directions can be a good way to describe what is happening. They may be willing to hear what you have to say. They may even be open to suggestions about how to make changes. More likely, they will not. Either way, you will have handled the situation in a mature and straightforward manner.

Unfortunately, this strategy does not work with family members and people at work with whom you have to interact. You do not have the ability to eliminate them from your life. For these energy vampires, you will need to establish boundaries so you can spend time together without allowing them to drive you crazy. Additionally, there may be friends or acquaintances you don't want to completely eliminate from your life; you just want them to stop taking so much from you. Boundaries are a great way to deal with both of these situations.

When faced with the prospect of setting boundaries, many people imagine that it will be a painful and contentious process. Well, I have a surprise for you. Most of the time, it is not that difficult. While we assume others will resist our efforts to set some limits, this generally doesn't turn out to be true. I have found that people actually appreciate it when we are honest and share our boundaries. How else will they know how we want to be treated? Since they cannot read our minds, we need to tell them.

To make the boundary-setting experience more successful, I have developed a few steps you can use to tame the energy vampires in your life:

♯ Inform the person that you have a boundary

This is really as simple as it sounds. It might go something like this: "I need to be honest with you and let you know that I don't appreciate it when you consistently show up late for our lunch dates."

♯ Identify the reason this boundary is important to you

While not required, it may help to briefly explain why this boundary is important to you. With the above example, you might want to remind the person that you only have an hour for lunch and you don't want to shortchange the conversation. Or, perhaps you can explain that you feel awkward and anxious having to sit alone for fifteen minutes, wondering whether he/she will show up. Most people get so caught up in their own life dramas that they fail to stop and consider the effect their behavior might have on other people.

♯ Request that the boundary be respected

Again, this can be quite simple. You can close the discussion by stating that you value the full hour together and asking them to make every effort to be punctual next time.

If someone does not honor your boundary, you may need to:

◻ Insist that the boundary be respected

Because others are not used to our setting and enforcing boundaries, this will be a process of educating and reminding people. Expect to issue several reminders at first. Be firm yet gentle, assuming the boundary infringements are due to forgetfulness and are not intentional.

◻ Identify the consequence if they keep ignoring your boundary

For the more chronic and willful violations, you will need to escalate the consequences. For me, this has been necessary in situations with family and friends who tell racist or sexist jokes in my presence. The first couple of times, I don't laugh and I explain that I don't find that kind of joke funny. If the behavior continues, I ask them not to tell such jokes around me. If they persist, especially in my own home, I may ask them to leave.

◻ Implement the consequence as a last resort

You must be willing to take the action that you have outlined. This is probably the biggest reason boundaries are ignored—when push comes to shove, we often back down and fail to follow through on the consequences. We seem to be so preoccupied with having people like us that we will endure blatant boundary violations. Seething inside with anger and resentment, we keep quiet in order to avoid hurting someone's feelings.

An additional thought to keep in mind is to try to remove the emotional charge from the boundary conversation. You want to be heard and to be taken seriously. A quivering voice and tears will weaken your message, as will a barrage of personal attacks and accusations. You have to stay focused on what you need and how the offending behavior affects you.

The best way to do this is to use "I" statements. Keep the focus on the impact the behavior has on you. Avoid sounding judgmental or accusatory. The issue is not whether the behavior is right or wrong, but rather what effect it has on you. Try not to take people's reactions personally. Even if you truly come from the place of trying to educate them about what you need to be your best, they may be insulted or angry. That is their problem, not yours. You are entitled to build your energy reserve by protecting yourself from these energy vampires.

- *Clear out the physical and emotional clutter in your life*

The other main energy drain that robs us of space in our lives is clutter. Think of the physical and emotional distractions you frequently bump into that steal your energy. Think of the big items in your life that are unfinished and/or unresolved. Clutter ranges from unorganized piles of papers on a desk and unfinished craft projects to unresolved emotional wounds and unscheduled medical check-ups. I bet just thinking about it causes you to feel anxious and depressed, with a definite outward loss of energy.

It is amazing how much clutter we tolerate in our lives. Fortunately, you can take affirmative steps to remove the clutter in your life and build up your reserve of time and energy. The best way to start to de-clutter your life is to own up to your clutter. Watch for those incomplete, festering items that you spend time worrying and stewing about, but not finishing or resolving. To identify your clutter, start by looking for the "un" items in your life, such as:

- unfinished projects
- unorganized paperwork
- uncomfortable surroundings
- unscheduled medical appointments
- unresolved feelings
- unproductive thoughts (jealousy, shame, guilt)
- unhealthy relationships

Clutter will generally appear in four areas of your life: your physical surroundings (home, work, and car), your finances, your relationships, and your health. Clutter is subjective. My clutter may not be your clutter. If it irritates you, causes anxiety, makes you feel like a failure, and drains your energy, then it's clutter.

Why is a de-cluttering process such an important part of a life do-over? Because clutter zaps your energy, making you feel guilty and inadequate. It is also a huge time waster. Consider the hours spent looking for lost items among piles of stuff or dwelling on unresolved feelings and emotions. But most importantly, allowing piles of clutter to remain in your life sends a failure message to your mind. If you can't even finish your sewing project, how can you possibly tackle a life do-over project? These negative messages are reinforced each time you look at or think about your clutter.

Conversely, when you jump in and tackle your clutter, you are signaling to yourself and the Universe that you are ready to receive more. You have demonstrated that you are a good steward over what you have, and you are ready to pursue your YES List. Without the distractions of your clutter, you can focus on the life path you would really like to follow.

Just by following this first step and identifying the clutter in your life, you will make significant progress towards reducing that clutter. The mind is an amazing tool. By placing something into the conscious realm of thought, solutions will begin to manifest themselves. This will seem almost effortless — a sure sign that good things are happening.

For even greater progress in your de-cluttering efforts, set aside some time to brainstorm several possible ways to clear up your clutter items. Try asking for suggestions from other people. Often we have dealt with a particular bit of clutter for so long that we just can't see all of the options for clearing it out. Other people could provide a fresh perspective and some great solutions. The more options you give yourself, the greater your chances of successfully eliminating this pesky clutter from your life.

After identifying several possible solutions, commit to one of them and take action. Finish it, face it, organize it, deal with it, toss it out, or heal it. At some point, you just have to go for it. Start with the easier items on your list, as this will create positive momentum and keep you going toward the more difficult clutter.

A great strategy for ensuring success is to find ways to be accountable to someone else. It is remarkable how much we can accomplish when we know we'll be checking in with another person. While we might find it hard to self-motivate and tackle the clutter by ourselves, we seem to be able to get the job done when the alternative is admitting to another person that we have failed. Given this propensity to stay on track when having to report to someone, I recommend finding a clutter-buster partner. This could be a supportive friend, family member, or even co-worker. Give yourself a clutter elimination deadline and share it with your partner. Ask them to check on you, either by phone or by e-mail. You'll be surprised at how much more committed you are when you know someone else will be asking for a progress report!

I used this accountability system to keep myself on track when writing this book. I made sure to tell several key people that my book was in process and that I wanted to finish the first draft of the manuscript by the end of the summer. Whenever I saw those friends, they would inquire about the book. It helped so much to have that regular check-in system in place. I am sure you'll find your clutter-buster buddy very helpful, and before long you will have reclaimed the energy you have been losing to your clutter.

If you are finding your clutter to be fairly well under control right now, here are a few suggestions to consider for extra credit in the battle against clutter. These will help you free up even more energy that you can use to make your YES List happen.

¤ Pack up those old magazines and toss out or give away every single one

¤ Face your fear of someone seeing your clutter and call a friend for help in getting rid of it and getting organized

¤ Roll your loose change and donate half to a worthwhile cause

¤ Defragment your computer's hard drive, or ask someone who knows how to do it to help

¤ Go through your old tax/financial records and throw away what you no longer need

¤ Call the dentist or the doctor and make that appointment for a certain test or check-up

¤ Give up an unrealistic goal you torment yourself with every year

Remember to Fill Up Your Internal Gas Tank

So far, we have been addressing the gaping holes that may exist in your internal gas tank, causing your energy to gush out. These are certainly the most important places to look to determine where your energy is going. Unless and until you deal with these major energy drains, you will never be able to have the kind of life you have dreamed of living.

However, even when you deal with the energy vampires in your life and stay vigilant about removing clutter, this will not guarantee a reserve of energy. The inevitable stresses and strains of daily life deplete a portion of energy each and every day. It is just a fact of life. This means you will want to find ways to replenish your energy — ways to refill your internal gas tank. Below are several suggestions that I have found to be very helpful and enjoyable.

- *Indulge in self-care activities on a regular basis*

These are the activities that make you feel good, nourished, replenished, and rejuvenated. I find a brisk walk outdoors, breathing in lots of fresh air, to be one of the best self-care activities. Not only does this make my body feel better, but it also improves my mental outlook. I can almost feel the negative energy leaving my body with each step I take. This can be a great thing to do on your lunch hour if you work indoors. Other ideas for taking care of yourself include a bubble bath, a pedicure/manicure/facial, a massage, and a little extra rest. I actually love to take a mid-afternoon catnap, especially if I have lots to do in the late afternoon or evening. Find your own ways of taking extra special care of yourself, and you'll feel your energy levels rising each time you enjoy these activities.

- *Create a community of positive, loving people*

Just as the energy vampires deplete our energy, positive and loving people replenish our energy. In order to tap into this wonderful way to recharge your battery, look for the right people to be part of your community. Consciously seek out the kinds of people you want to have as friends — people who are on the personal development path, open to new ideas, committed to honest communication, and easy to be around. The clearer your intentions are about the kinds of friends you want to have in your life, the greater the chance that you will find those kinds of people and gain their love and support.

• *Develop a practice that connects you with your heart and soul*

Inside each one of us is an amazing source of energy that is often left largely untapped—our heart and soul. We get so caught up in our thoughts and mental processes that we forget to connect with the part of ourselves that is separate from our ego and self-focused obsessions. One of the things I really like about the Alcoholics Anonymous program is how it teaches the importance of connecting with the Higher Power, whatever that looks like for each person. In writing and speaking about this connection to our heart and soul, I use various words. God, Source, Love, Mother Nature, and Universe are all possibilities. Whatever you feel comfortable with is fine. Just develop some practice that allows you to connect with your deepest self and spiritual source.

I know these suggestions will help you create more room for you in your life. When you get a handle on where you are squandering your time, how you are giving your energy to others, and what you can do to keep your internal gas tank full, you'll be making big strides in opening up space for your life do-over. And, until you do, you'll stay stuck in neutral, too overwhelmed to seriously consider a new path for your life.

> *Be who you are and say what you feel, because those who*
> *mind don't matter and those who matter don't mind.*
>
> —Dr. Seuss

Strategy #5
Conquer Your
Fears and Doubts

I am an old man now and I have known many troubles,
and most of them have never come to pass.

—Mark Twain

Although finding the time and energy to focus on the changes you would like to make in your life is a big challenge, by far the biggest obstacle to redesigning your life path is the collection of fears and doubts that plague your mind and emotions. I wish I could tell you there is a magic cure for these tenacious worries and negative beliefs, but I have not found one. However, I have discovered that it is possible to manage your fears and doubts by recognizing them and choosing not to give them your power and attention. Over time, you will find their hold on you lessening, and you will be able to move forward in life despite their predictions of certain doom and gloom.

I can help you with this process by sharing what I have learned about wrestling with the fear monsters and by showing you how to tackle the insidious rumblings of self-doubt. It is definitely not an event, but rather a process of getting to know your specific fears and finding concrete tools you can use when they surface. I suggest focusing on:

> ➤ How to better understand the concepts of fear and doubt
> ➤ Strategies for conquering your fears by identifying them and taking away their power
> ➤ Strategies for conquering your doubts by developing new beliefs about yourself and your world and finding the evidence to support those new beliefs

Understanding the Concepts of Fear and Doubt

An important first step is to take a closer look at these similar concepts of fear and doubt. While they are very connected, I have discovered important differences between the two. Fears are the negative and scary emotional responses we feel in our hearts and in our guts. A small percentage of our fears are healthy and productive, such as a fear of ferocious wild animals or of crazy criminals wielding dangerous weapons. Thank goodness our internal systems are hard-wired to recognize these external sources of danger and protect us from injury.

Unfortunately, most of our fears are not this helpful. They are based on irrational yet powerful misconceptions about our true potential and ourselves. Some of the most common things people are afraid of are failure, rejection, disapproval, poverty, intimacy, change, and of course, death. Specific activities can also be the source of fears, such as public speaking, flying, or talking to new people.

These types of fears come from a variety of sources. They may be a legacy from our parents, a result of childhood trauma, or a consequence of negative life experiences. In the extreme, they manifest themselves as crippling phobias requiring treatment from trained professionals in the field of psychotherapy and/or psychiatry. For most people, they are the reason for staying stuck in neutral and resisting positive life changes.

One of the big fear issues I had to wrestle with during my life do-over was the feeling that something bad would happen if I took a risk and changed my life. I know this came from my family dynamics, as my mother was frequently very ill, and bad things did happen a lot when I was a child. Fortunately, I came to the point where my need to follow the real me was stronger than this fear, and I had to reckon with being afraid of change in order to have the life I really wanted.

Doubts, on the other hand, are the mind games that we play based on our distorted view of the world. Our thoughts, rather than our emotions, are the favorite location for doubts. Perhaps you recognize one or more of these common self-doubts:

• *There is not enough for everyone—I need to cling to my few crumbs*

• *I am not good enough*

• *I am not lovable, especially if people know the real me*

• *I am not attractive*

• *Strangers represent danger and should be avoided*

• *I will get hurt if I get close to people and open myself up to them*

At one of my recent workshops focusing on this very topic, a woman shared the negative mindset that plagued her. As a little girl, she never felt like she was good enough to gain her father's approval. She tried very hard to do everything her father wanted, and responded to all of his needs so that he would approve of her. As an adult, she realized this was significantly affecting her behavior with her manager at work, as she could feel herself slipping into this old behavior pattern. Whenever she received negative feedback on her job performance, she was not able to respond rationally, but rather felt herself become that little girl once again, desperately seeking to gain approval. By recognizing this limiting belief, she was able to stop the destructive pattern and address her manager's concerns without becoming so emotionally charged.

You may be wondering what comes first, the emotional response of fear, which then develops into a distorted view of the world, or the doubting thought, which triggers the feeling of fear? I suppose this question has preoccupied scientific researchers for quite a long time. But I think it is a lot like asking which came first, the chicken or the egg? The reality is that both exist and are serious obstacles to making changes and moving forward. That is why I have developed techniques to manage both our fears and our doubts.

Strategies for Conquering Your Fears

The most important step in dealing with your fears is to get to know them. You will be able to eliminate a great extent of their hold over you when you recognize them and choose not to embrace the lies they whisper into your heart. This process of recognizing your fears involves knowing the following information about each one of them:

- *When does it come to you*
- *What does it say*
- *What other voices does it use*
- *What memories does it drag up*
- *What is the core fear—the fear that is behind most of the other fears*

For example, one of my fears is that of failure. It usually comes to me in the middle of the night when I wake up and start worrying about whether I will be successful in my next project. This fear likes to tell me that I am not working hard enough or that my expectations are unrealistic. It likes to make me start worrying about how I will face other people in my life when I crash and burn. This is my core fear after I peel away the outer layers. If I let myself, I can go into a very distressing downward spiral that gets my heart pounding and causes me to break into a cold sweat.

What I have discovered is that the sooner I recognize this fear, the sooner I can laugh at it and shake it off. By knowing what is happening, I can choose not to let myself get caught up in the lies. This is critical. We need to resist the temptation to get caught up in the crazy-making of our fears. Quick action is needed to prevent the fear from taking hold of our emotional well-being.

In order to take action, we need to have a set of tools ready to use to dislodge the fear. I suggest assembling a "fear tool kit" at some time other than when you are in the middle of a fear attack. Think about what will work in your fear battles. I find it is very helpful to stock my bedside drawer with a pad of paper, a pen, a few inspirational readings, and a small flashlight. When the failure fear comes in the middle of the night, I write down my fears, which prompts me to admit how crazy they are. Then I read a few passages from my positive thought books to get me out of the fear zone. The flashlight is useful so that I don't have to turn on the bedroom light and wake up my husband. By being prepared, I can stop the fear spiral before it takes hold.

Additionally, I have developed a visualization that I often use when my fears cry out at me in the dark. I imagine a large, loving being who is seated and welcomes me into his lap. I actually visualize a form much like the beautiful and powerful white marble statue of Abraham Lincoln at the Lincoln Memorial in Washington, D.C. This may sound a bit weird, but it really works for me. He holds me and asks me to release my fears and worries to him, at least for the rest of the night. There is something about this wise and loving being that makes me feel safe and well taken care of. When I awaken the next morning, I rarely remember to retrieve my concerns.

Another tool to prevent your fears from growing roots in your psyche is to starve your fears and feed your dreams. Notice how long you are allowing yourself to dwell in the place of fear and worry. It is amazing how much time during the day can be spent in the fear zone. If you find you just cannot give up your worry time, try limiting yourself to twenty minutes a day. Set a timer and let yourself do all the fretting and worrying you want to do. Really give it a go—come up with your juiciest fears and wallow in them for a full twenty minutes. Then for the rest of the day, when you are tempted to go back into the fear zone, stop yourself and remember that you can revisit that concern tomorrow during your twenty-minute worry segment.

Equally as important as limiting your fear time is expanding your dream time. The key is to spend at least as much time immersed in your exciting dreams, passions, and pursuits as you do with your negative and destructive fears. Since you are now paying attention to how much time you are spending with your fears, you will know how much time you need to spend feeding your dreams. The goal is to spend a lot more time with your dreams than you do with your fears. While this may seem difficult at first, as you reduce the amount of fear time, you will have more quality time to spend with your dreams and desires.

A final tactic you may want to use in managing your fears is to play the "what-if" game. I have found that quite often, our fears seem much worse to us than they are in reality. While we may think we will have a heart attack and die if we have to speak in front of people, that won't actually happen. So for instance, if public speaking is one of your fears, ask yourself, "What is the worst thing that could happen to me if I got up and spoke?" You might say that you would open your mouth and nothing would come out. Okay, so what if that happens? You would simply walk away from the podium. You would not die, you would not be thrown in jail, and you would not become an outcast from society. You would suffer a bit of an ego bruising and move on with your day. Your friends and family would still love and support you. In fact, most people in the audience would be sympathetic and encourage you to try again. The worst-case scenario would not be anywhere close to what you had imagined.

I found this strategy to be very useful when I was looking at the possibility of walking away from being a lawyer. I asked myself what would happen if I did not find a new and more fulfilling career, or if I was not successful at my new career. I realized that my answer to "what if I failed" was that I would go back to being a lawyer. My worst-case scenario was to return to the life I was then living. Suddenly, my new choices did not seem as scary as I was imagining in my dark, fearful moments.

It is very important to keep in mind that people who do exciting, courageous things in their lives do not wait to do those things until they have no fear. As the saying goes, they feel the fear and do it anyway. They are aware of their fears and consciously decide not to let those fears rule their lives. They really understand Ambrose Redmon's observation that "courage is not the absence of fear, but rather the judgment that something else is more important than fear."

Until you get to know your fears and develop your own process for eliminating their hold over you, chances are you will remain a hostage to their powers of inertia. Moreover, you will miss the opportunity to live the life you really want, and are entitled, to live.

Strategies for Conquering Your Doubts

Now we'll turn our attention to the negative, limiting thought processes that make up your self-doubts. These can actually be more difficult to manage than your fears because you may not even realize what they are. Unlike fears, which you feel in your body when they are trying to take hold, your doubts may be so much a part of your worldview that you can't see past them. This means you need to be able to step outside the box, question your views and beliefs about how the world works, and decide which ones are serving you well and which are not.

Engaging in this process requires you to be at least a little bit open-minded and willing to look at your mental framework. Many people are quite reluctant to undertake this type of belief inventory. They will let their lives continue to go nowhere rather than rock the boat. Or, they will let other people dictate what they should believe rather than explore what makes sense for them. This type of apathetic thinking may seem safe and secure, but it leads to a life lacking in authenticity and meaning. As the ancient philosopher Plato wrote, "An unexamined life is not worth living."

During a recent episode of Dr. Phil's weight-loss challenge, he shared a very helpful tool for discovering the hidden limiting beliefs that are lurking in our minds and waiting to sabotage our successes in life. He asked the participants to write down the story they would tell themselves in a few months if they failed to reach their weight-loss goals. The responses included, "I am lazy and undisciplined and don't ever accomplish my goals," "I am a bad person and I don't deserve the help I am receiving," and, "I won't be able to maintain my weight loss, so why should I even try?" You can see how each one of these failure explanations reveals a negative belief that casts serious doubts on being able to reach the weight-loss goals.

Try this exercise with your goal of designing and exploring a new path in life. If you don't make any real progress toward this goal in the next six months, what story will you tell yourself? Perhaps that focusing on your needs and wants is too self-centered? Or, that you don't deserve real happiness and fulfillment? Maybe even that life is meant to be difficult, and suffering is part of the process? These stories will shed light on the beliefs that are at the root of your doubts and negative self-talk.

Once you have identified the self-doubts and limiting beliefs you have about yourself and the world around you, ask yourself whether those thought patterns have served you well so far in your life. Have they allowed you to move confidently in the direction of your dreams, or have they held you back? Do they help you trust yourself and others, or do they produce doubt and fear? What life choices have you made based on your mental framework? Take some time to collect and analyze this information.

If you decide that your beliefs are leading you to doubt yourself and your potential, consider whether a particular belief has to be true for you. What is the origin of this belief? What would happen if you altered this thought process? What do other people believe about the same concept? What does the concrete evidence in your life tell you about what is actually true for you? You may be surprised to learn how far your doubts and negative beliefs are from reality.

This seems to be especially true of thoughts and beliefs about money. How many people do you know who have plenty of money in the bank and numerous secure investments, yet act as if they were one step away from poverty? Their erroneous beliefs tell them that they do not have enough, and their money could disappear. Certainly, people who lived through the 1929 stock market crash and the Great Depression had very persuasive evidence to support this view of fear and lack. But how unfortunate that they cannot get past that experience to see their current prosperity.

One of the big doubts that I had to face during my life do-over involved my belief that I needed a steady weekly paycheck in order to have financial security. I doubted whether I could provide enough income with my new life-coaching business. When I asked myself what other people believe about being self-employed, and what alternative thought process I could adopt, I decided to experiment with a different mindset. I reshaped my negative belief into a more encouraging one, namely that I am a multi-talented woman pursuing a fuller expression of my gifts, supported by God/Spirit/Universe. Just writing down this alternative belief felt very freeing and encouraging.

The real shift for me came when I began to look for concrete examples of how this new belief was actually true in my life. I gave myself permission to fully accept that I do have gifts and talents to share with the world. As I acknowledged this truth, wonderful income opportunities began to open up for me. With increasing evidence of my ability to make money in this career, my new belief has become stronger and stronger, and I find the nagging voice of doubt becoming much weaker. It still surfaces occasionally, but once I recognize it and remind myself that it is no longer my truth, it seems to fade away quite quickly.

I encourage you to try on a new belief and see what happens. As you make an honest effort to reshape your thought processes, you will be presented with amazing affirmations to support and encourage you in this endeavor. Moreover, as the evidence piles up, your new belief will grow stronger and stronger and overshadow the lingering doubts that pop up from time to time. You will understand Whoopi Goldberg's revelation, "It never occurs to me that there are things that I cannot do."

This reminds me of the story about the realtor who was showing a home to a young couple. The wife said she found her current neighbors to be generally meddlesome and intrusive, and wondered if that was true in this area as well. The realtor replied that it was. When another couple asked to see the same home, that wife said she thought her current neighbors were very nice and pleasant to live near. She wondered if that was true in this neighborhood as well. The realtor responded that it was. You see, each of these women had a set belief about neighbors, and the realtor knew they would find what they were looking for. The realtor agreed with the wise words of archaeologist John Lubbock, "What we see depends mainly on what we look for."

Our doubts can definitely dictate how we view the world and what we find showing up in our lives. As we learn to reframe and reshape our beliefs about the outside world, we will find evidence to support our new beliefs and prevent our doubts from dictating our life choices. With our fears and doubts in check, we can make clearer decisions and chart a truer life course.

Handling our fears is part of the tapestry of a life well-lived.

—Susan Jeffers

Strategy #6
Resign as
Master of the Universe

Learn to let go — that is the key to happiness.

—The Buddha

This final strategy is actually optional. You can complete your life do-over without learning how to take your hands off the controls and go with the flow of life. You can continue to juggle all of the balls yourself and work very hard, pushing and straining to make your do-over a reality. The problem is that by trying to maintain the illusion of control, you will deprive yourself of the guidance and assistance that can make your journey so much easier and infinitely more enjoyable. I have tried it both ways, and I am convinced that being a co-creator with the Universe is a much wiser approach than trying to be the master.

These two approaches to getting things done in life are best described as willpower vs. flow power. Willpower is the push, exert, make-it-happen way of handling life changes and reaching goals. In contrast, flow power is about allowing, removing resistance, and embracing whatever shows up. In many ways, willpower is like the strength and resolve required to paddle a canoe upstream, whereas flow power is more like the ease and surrender experienced while traveling with the river's sure and steady current.

When I was developing my coaching business, I had a chance to look at both of these options. I knew that I could approach building my business with the same mindset that I had used while building my legal career. I could create a plan with a detailed to-do list for each day and work very hard at finding clients. As I was sharing this approach with my life coach, Margaret Krigbaum, she raised the possibility of another way. Her suggestion was that I take action every day without planning it all out ahead of time. Instead, I could ask myself each day what I felt like doing, what opportunities were presenting themselves to me, and what felt easy. Hmmm? Could this really be possible? I was willing to give it a try.

What I discovered was the joy and magic that comes from allowing life to unfold each day and from welcoming divine assistance. With this shift in my thinking, I realized that my old way of getting things done was effective, but very draining and often difficult. This new approach seemed to be working just as well, without the angst and fatigue that came with trying to figure everything out ahead of time and muscle my way through life. I was having fun in this new endeavor and was amazed at the doors that were opening up for me without having to be forced open.

When I share this story with others, I often encounter quite a bit of skepticism. We are so programmed to believe life must be hard and difficult, that we reject the notion of an easier way. Plus, the idea of giving up the controls and asking for help and guidance requires us to check our egos at the door. We need to be willing to see different perspectives and admit that we don't have all of the answers. I have found this to be more than an even trade for the incredible variety of options that open up for us once we loosen our grip on the controls of life.

I know this may sound like "hocus-pocus" and you may not be convinced about what I'm presenting. Let's make a deal. Read through the following tools and suggestions for resigning as Master of the Universe. Try one of them during the next week. See what happens. What do you have to lose? You just might find there is some truth behind these strategies:

> Recognize and follow your wise, inner voice
> Use the Law of Attraction
> Do what you feel like doing
> Expect assistance from unexpected sources
> Be flexible and dance with what shows up

As you read these ideas, you may find yourself thinking that they sound quite simple and easy. I would partially agree with you. The ideas are easy to grasp. You do not need to be a rocket scientist to understand them. However, they are not necessarily simple to implement in your life. Because our society is so firmly rooted in the notion of hard work and struggle, it can be quite difficult at first to follow these strategies for doing less and relinquishing the controls. This is to be expected when you are bucking the established system. But stick with it! You will quickly see the tremendous benefits that come from allowing life to happen instead of making it fit your rigid specifications.

Recognize and Follow Your Wise, Inner Voice

You have been provided with an amazing navigational tool for choosing and following a new life course with ease and confidence. It is your wise, inner voice that serves as your internal radar. You know what I am describing. Just think of a time in life when you had a decision to make, and you ignored your wise, inner voice. While you were making the wrong choice, you heard this voice trying to persuade you to choose differently. I bet that afterwards, you even admitted knowing, deep in your gut, that your choice was a mistake. This was your wise, inner self, trying to get your attention.

Even though it is easy to recognize after the fact, it is not always easy to recognize that voice when you are in the midst of a life decision. I am frequently asked how to distinguish the wise, inner voice from all the other voices competing for our attention, especially when we are trying to make a difficult choice. During my life do-over, I learned several things about the wise, inner voice that will help you recognize and trust its guidance.

• *First and foremost, it always looks out for your best interests*

In contrast to the other voices that have their own agendas, your wise, inner voice connects you to your true self. Its sole function is to provide you with love, fulfillment, and a sense of well-being. So, take a look at what agenda the voice is advocating, and decide if it is looking out for what is right for you.

• *Second, it will get your attention*

The ideas and opportunities your wise, inner voice encourages you to pursue will get your attention. They will probably be bigger and better than you think are possible for yourself, and they will most certainly interest you. When considering these exciting options, you will feel truly alive and excited about what your life could be like. Your wise, inner voice is directly connected to your heart and knows how to make you see, and feel, what is truly possible for your life.

• *Third, it won't go away no matter how much you try to ignore it*

It will repeat its advice, getting louder and clearer each time. Eventually, it may have to resort to drastic measures to get your attention, but it will not rest until you take notice. I know this is why some people end up with physical and emotional breakdowns. They ignore the warnings of their inner voice to slow down and take care of themselves, until they end up flat on their backs. That is the only way they will listen. You can avoid these drastic situations by learning to recognize the sound of your wise, inner voice early, when it uses a gentle nudge instead of a knock upside the head.

The most effective way to listen to your wise, inner voice is to create some room in your life for quiet time. You will never hear your true guidance if your life is filled with the din of constant do-ing-ness and busy-ness. Meditation works well for some people. A quiet walk in nature is another possibility. Still others find a bathtub and a locked bathroom door work wonders. I love to simply sit out back on my deck and watch the birds and lizards play in my garden while the white clouds dance in the turquoise blue sky.

The key is to find some time when you are doing nothing. See what ideas and feelings come to the surface of your mind. Listen to your intuitive feelings. If you are facing a particular decision, ask your wise, inner self for help, for a clue or a signal. Then be prepared to receive your direction, for it will surely come to you, either at that moment or later in your day.

Once you can identify your wise, inner voice, you need to trust its suggestions and take action. So often, I hear people explain that they knew the right steps to take, but they just didn't move forward. One of the biggest reasons for this hesitation is that we do not get all of the pieces to the puzzle at once. We receive just enough to get us going down the right path, but we can't always see the final destination. This means we have to develop our trust muscle—we must get to the place of knowing that our wise, inner voice has our best interests in mind and will not lead us astray. This gets easier to do the more you do it, because you can remind yourself of the amazing results you enjoyed when you trusted this voice in the past.

Another reason you may be tempted to ignore your wise, inner voice is that it may not seem rational or logical to you or to the people around you. Can you imagine how it sounded to me when I got clear on the message to leave my legal career and pursue my gifts and talents, not knowing how I would be able to make a living doing it? I did not discover the profession of life coaching until nine months after I took the seemingly irrational step of quitting my job. Of course, my wise, inner voice knew this would be the ultimate direction that I would take. I am so glad I found the ability to trust, even though I could not see the end of the road at that time.

I love Jonas Salk's admission about how much he relied on his innate wisdom. "It is always with excitement that I wake up in the mornings wondering what my intuition will toss to me, like gifts from the sea. I work with it and rely on it. It's my partner." I couldn't agree more.

Use the Law of Attraction

Most people have a vague idea about the Law of Attraction. We often hear phrases such as "like attracts like" or "as a man thinketh, so goes his life." Yet most people fail to grasp the incredible truth embodied in these sayings. Once we understand the real power contained in the Law of Attraction and set about to harness this power in our lives, we gain a valuable tool for effortlessly manifesting all that we want and need in life.

So, what is this Law of Attraction? We can begin with the simplest explanation, which is that we manifest our dominant thoughts. What we focus on and put our emotions behind is what we bring into our lives, because the Universe gets the message and sets about to make it happen. This explains why people who have a positive and optimistic outlook on life generally have good luck, while those who always look for the negative side of life tend to find bad luck. Our thoughts are just like a big magnet, drawing more of the same to us.

Think of it this way. Your mind simply says "yes" to whatever you put into it. If you put in the idea that you have abundance and prosperity, your mind says "yes" to that thought and sets about to create more. If on the other hand, you focus on what is missing and the perceived scarcity in your life, your mind says "yes" and manifests more lack. Your mind, and the energy flow that takes its cue from your mind, do not screen or judge your thoughts and intentions. They simply set about to make them real.

The Law of Attraction is a universal law that works regardless of whether or not you are aware of it or believe in its incredible power. It is as impersonal and unchanging as the Law of Gravity. If you jump off a building, you will fall down. This is true even if you have never heard of the concept of gravity or think it is a foolish idea. The Law of Attraction works the same way. It has been at work your whole life, and will continue to be a guiding force even if you don't want to accept it as true.

Given the inevitable presence of the Law of Attraction, why not take advantage of it and tap into this amazing magnetic principle?

In studying and applying the concept, I have learned several methods for using it to bring what I want and need into my life. When I share these with clients and ask them to experiment with the Law of Attraction, I hear amazing stories of how their intentions manifested. I encourage you to try these.

• *Set your intentions with clarity, detail, and emotion*

I want to give you a warning here—be careful what you ask for. When you take the time to focus on the resources and assistance you would like to receive, and then form this into a clear intention, you will bring it into your life. This is even more powerful when you put your energy and emotion behind the intention. You send out a very strong vibration into the Universe, which if not cancelled by contrary intentions, will materialize in your life. So take some time to create a detailed picture of what you want to bring into your life, get excited and enthusiastic about it, and watch it come to be.

• *Don't try to control the "How"— let the Universe do the work*

This is the big stumbling block. In order for the Law of Attraction to work, you have to be willing to let it happen. You cannot try to control the details of how your intentions will come into your life. It is impossible to be open to the full range of possibilities and at the same time make all of the plans and arrangements. This is the letting go part, and it is very challenging for most people. When you find yourself getting anxious and wanting to know the how, when, where, and who, take a deep breath and let go of your expectations. Instead, remind yourself that the Universe has this matter fully handled, and redirect your thoughts and emotions to visualizing and getting excited about your intention.

• *Don't cancel your intentions with fear and contrary thoughts*

When you are not receiving what you believe to be your set intentions, it is usually because you have cancelled them out with contrary thoughts that are more powerful. Think about it. If you spend ten minutes setting your intention, and then four hours doubting that it will come to you, which thought will prevail? Of course, the dominant thought of fear and doubt. The Law of Attraction is providing you with exactly what you have been focusing upon, but you are actually focusing on the wrong thing. The trick is to take an honest look at your beliefs and intentions, and then decide if you want to make some changes. You may even want to re-read the section in Strategy #4 about conquering your fears and doubts if you find they have reappeared and started to grow new roots into your psyche.

Do What You Feel Like Doing

I am a very organized and disciplined person. My natural tendency is to create to-do lists and stick to them regardless of whether or not I am enjoying what I am doing. Although this does result in my getting the work done, I often feel restless and resentful at having to do work that I really don't want to do. This leads to my pursuing the work almost absent-mindedly, without feeling much positive energy or joy about what I am doing. I simply plod along.

In the past few years, I have directly challenged this approach to getting things done. I've discovered the sense of ease and happiness that comes from doing what I feel like doing, rather than what I think I should be doing or what I have assigned as my tasks for the day. I've uncovered a whole new rhythm to the day that lets me accomplish all of my tasks with much more energy and success than I achieved when I forced myself to do set things each day. It has become my new mantra and guidepost for my work.

Doing what I feel like doing has led to two significant changes to my workday. I have abandoned my daily to-do list in favor of a weekly to-do list. Each day when I wake up, I review my weekly to-do list and ask myself what I feel like doing that day. Of course, there are days when I have set appointments, so I do need to honor those commitments. However, for the remaining unscheduled time, I do what I want to do. Some days I really do feel like making calls, talking to people, and being outgoing. Other days I feel like holing up in my office and spending time on the computer. I find that I do get everything done by the end of the week, but now it is with a smile and a sense of ease.

I know what you are thinking. If you gave yourself permission to do only what you felt like doing, there are certain tasks that you would never get to. I have heard this many times from my clients when I ask them to try the weekly to-do list. My response is two-fold. My first suggestion is to try the weekly to-do list for a few weeks and see if that is really true. I have found that as my mood and energy levels ebb and flow during the week, things that sound unpleasant or difficult one day really do seem interesting on other days. Follow your internal gauge and focus on doing only what feels fun and joyful. I think you will be surprised at how productive you will be and how much more enjoyable your work will seem.

If after trying this for a few weeks, you do find your list is full of things you never feel like doing, then why are they on your to-do list? Perhaps you need to look at your job/career/profession with a more critical eye. Doing tasks day after day that you don't really *want* to do takes a tremendous toll on your physical and emotional well-being. I know this only too well. This can be a clear signal that it's time to seriously consider making better life choices.

One of my favorite ways to follow this concept of doing what I feel like doing is to take a "ME Day" at least once a month. This is a day when I make no set plans. My only goal for the day is to do, in each moment, what brings me joy and what I truly want to do. Sometimes this means staying in my pajamas and reading a novel. Other times, I may take a hike or go shopping. I have even felt like cleaning up the house or organizing my office files. What I do is not as important as following my heart and giving myself permission to do only what I feel like doing.

The benefits of this ME Day are numerous. It helps me connect to my passions, interests, and desires, which can be neglected in the busy pace of normal life. Additionally, it allows me a full day of rest and relaxation, an opportunity to recharge my battery. And, of course, it provides me with lots of free time to listen to my wise, inner voice.

Taking a 24-hour ME Day is one of my favorite assignments for clients that are stressed out and/or way overcommitted. As much as they think they will enjoy this day, most of them report that it is actually quite difficult to do. They find it very hard to resist the temptation to do what they should do or to schedule lots of activities for that day. Some even report feeling bored or restless, because they have forgotten how to live in the present moment. Once they allow themselves to slow down and follow their feelings, they realize how much more productive they are when they return to their busy schedules.

Does this sound intriguing to you? Are you willing to try doing more of what you feel like doing? I hope you will take this challenge and schedule a ME Day sometime very soon. It might just be the beginning of a whole new mindset about how to more fully enjoy your work and make it feel more like playtime.

Welcome Assistance from Unexpected Sources

As you begin to let go of the controls and allow your life to unfold, you will be provided with some wonderful assistance and guidance from unexpected sources. This is often referred to as "serendipity" or "synchronicity" — those apparently chance encounters that seem cosmically orchestrated. I have also heard this described as those moments when God performs a miracle and chooses to remain anonymous. I am sure you have experienced this assistance when just the right person calls you; the perfect book at the library catches your attention as you are looking through the shelves; or you learn about a very helpful community program to attend by browsing the newspaper.

One of my favorite quotations about the power of synchronicity comes from William Hutchinson Murray, the leader of the Scottish Himalayan Expedition that scaled Mt. Everest in 1951. He declared, "The moment one definitely commits oneself, than providence moves too. A whole stream of events issue from the decision, raising in one's favor all manner of unforeseen incidents, meetings, and material assistance which no man could have dreamt would come his way."

Sometimes we are so stuck on how the assistance should come into our lives that we fail to see the help coming our way. A great example of this is the tale of the man who was hiking a narrow river canyon when a rainstorm upstream caused the water level in the river to rise very quickly. A ranger came through the canyon and offered to guide the hiker to safety, but he declined, explaining that he was a man of faith and knew God would take care of him.

As the river continued to rise, a group in a canoe came by and offered to let the hiker join them and get to higher ground. Again, he said no thanks and reaffirmed his belief that God would take care of him. Finally, the water was swirling around his neck and the hiker could barely stay afloat. A helicopter pilot saw him and yelled for him to grab the dangling rescue rope. The hiker refused, yelling back that he was safe because God was looking out for him.

As the water filled the canyon, the hiker drowned and found himself in heaven facing God. The hiker was quite angry, accusing God of failing to protect him from the dangerous water even though he had repeatedly expressed his faith. God shook his head in disbelief and exclaimed, "I sent you the ranger, I sent you the canoe, I sent you the helicopter..."

Isn't this true? We get so fixated on our view of how life should unfold that we fail to see the assistance and opportunities coming our way every single day. Can you see how much easier life would be if we did not have to come up with all the solutions by ourselves? Consider the benefits of having a team of experienced and talented advisors at your disposal. I have found that is exactly what we have when we open up and allow the higher power to assist us.

One of my first experiences with this assistance occurred when I found Cheryl Richardson's book, *Take Time for Your Life,* at the bookstore. I was drawn to a different section of books from those I had originally intended to look through. Her book seemed to be almost glowing. I could not resist the temptation to pull it off the shelf. When I opened it, the pages fell to the exact spot where she described her frustrations with her accounting job and the joy she had found in the profession of life coaching. Wow! This was the precise message I needed to hear. I had not even heard of life coaching until I discovered that book, and it led me in a direction that I could never have imagined by myself.

You can increase the occurrence of synchronistic events in your life in several ways. Start by recognizing them when they come, and acknowledge the help and guidance. Being aware of this assistance and grateful for its presence will open up more room in your life for it to appear. If you are keeping a journal, I suggest you write down examples of unexpected guidance to help you remember its availability when you need some extra assistance. Another important tip is to know and respect the "rule of three." When you hear about something or someone three times, consider this a very strong message to follow up. Even one or two times are interesting to note, but three times is a sure signal to pay attention.

A final suggestion is to be aware when resistance shows up in your life. I have found that noticing when things are not working out can be a very valuable source of divine guidance. Perhaps this is not the right time or the right life choice for you. I heeded the resistance signal recently when deciding whether to buy a new house in a different part of town. Although the new home seemed perfect for me and my husband, we were not able to sell our current home, which we really wanted to do for the down payment.

We ultimately let go of the new house, and that has turned out to be a very wise decision. The new neighborhood is not what we thought it would be, and we would have been very unhappy in that environment. Plus, instead of buying a bigger home, we are now looking at getting a camper so we can get back to spending time on the open road. Thank goodness enough obstacles came our way so that we had to listen to the message behind the resistance.

Be Flexible and Dance with What Shows Up

Another important way to release our expectations and the need to control all of life's details is to cultivate flexibility, the ability to go with the flow and not get upset if things don't work out exactly as we had assumed they would. We need to remember, "Blessed are the flexible, for they shall not be bent out of shape." This is because in the big picture of life it doesn't really matter if we take some unexpected twists and turns. In fact, some of the best outcomes are often the result of unforeseen detours from our life plan.

I have a great example of the wonderful blessings that can come your way if you are willing to practice flexibility. When I was in my teens and creating my life plan, I decided not to get married until after finishing college and law school. I figured that I would have more options and enjoy life more if I was single while completing my education. Well, during the summer before my sophomore year in college, when I was just eighteen, I met the man, my future husband Jim, who would put a big wrinkle in those plans.

We started living together a few months after we met, and we have been together ever since. I can't imagine my life without him. Jim's love, support, and encouragement have been the keys to my joys and successes in life, and I can't imagine spending all those years without him. Good thing I was willing to renegotiate my plans to include this wonderful wrinkle!

At the heart of developing flexibility is the belief that there are no mistakes in life. When we look at unforeseen interruptions and deviations as opportunities to grow and learn, we can begin to welcome them into our lives instead of resisting and resenting them. Just because our plans go awry does not mean the big picture has been disrupted. There is so much truth in the observation by John Lennon, "Life is what happens to you while you're busy making other plans."

I recently saw the movie *Terminal* in which Tom Hanks plays a visitor to the United States from a fictitious Eastern European country. While he is flying to the United States, his country undergoes an internal revolution and his government revokes his visa. This means he cannot enter the United States nor can he return to his home country. He must remain in the international terminal at the airport in New York City until the situation can be resolved among the bureaucrats of the two countries. Talk about a change of plans!

What I really enjoyed about the movie is how this character deals with the situation. Rather than react by getting angry or yelling at the immigration officials, he is respectful and pleasant to everyone as he sets about making a living space for himself in an unused section of the airport terminal. He responds by creatively finding food, employment, and opportunities for friendships. He ends up teaching those around him some very important life lessons, and eventually his situation does get resolved. By embracing this unexpected set of circumstances, he moves forward in life and uses the opportunity to share his gifts with those around him.

We could all learn from this lesson. When life throws us what we perceive to be a curveball, we have two choices. We can react by getting angry, irritated, or frustrated. Or, we can respond by accepting what is, and trusting that there is a reason for the diversion. Some of the most interesting experiences of our lives come out of these unexpected changes to our plans.

The flexibility concept enhances all the other techniques for resigning as Master of the Universe. Our wise, inner voice comes through much clearer when we are willing to deviate from our plans. We tap into the Law of Attraction when we let go of our attachment to how, when, and where our resources will materialize. Our ability to respond to change is greatly increased when we let go of rigid schedules and begin to enjoy the synchronistic events and messages that surprise us during the day. Cultivating flexibility is the key to enjoying the life do-over journey.

> *You have to strive every minute to get rid of the life that you have planned in order to have the life that's waiting to be yours.*
>
> —Joseph Campbell

Conclusion

Your Best Life
Is Waiting for You

Find your true path. It is so easy to become someone we
don't want to be, without even realizing it's happening.

—Bernie Siegel, M.D.

The essence of the life do-over process involves removing from your life what isn't working and embracing the real you that is buried under a mountain of forgotten dreams and poor life choices. Much like Michelangelo's statue of David was waiting to be released from the block of marble, your best life is also waiting to be uncovered. You just need to remove the excess marble that has built up over the years and hidden the real you. Once you do, you will be able to design a new path in life that will take you where you want to go—to a more authentic life that feels absolutely right for you.

The real tragedy would be to get to the end of your life and realize, too late, that you missed opportunities, failed to follow your dreams, and deprived the world of your gifts. My message is to take a close look at this question: What would you do differently if you had your life to live over? Then make new choices that will lead to the life you really want and are meant to live. As you ponder this question, keep the following suggestions in mind:

> ➤ Schedule regular time to work on your life
> ➤ Revisit the life do-over strategies as needed
> ➤ Develop a life do-over support system
> ➤ Enjoy the journey

Schedule Regular Time to Work on Your Life

Although I have mentioned this several times already, it bears repeating. You will not make any real progress in redirecting your life unless you stop the day-to-day activities and take some time to work on your life. Just wanting things to change is not enough. As Albert Einstein so wisely observed, "The definition of insanity is doing the same thing over and over again and expecting different results." Your new life path is waiting for you, but you need to do some things differently, which means developing a strategic plan for making new life choices. This requires an investment of time and energy.

I am confident you will really enjoy this time for yourself. Since you have taken the time to read this book, I assume you're interested in learning to live from the inside out, to connect with and make time for the real you, to deal with your fears and doubts, and to resign as Master of the Universe. Given this eagerness to explore a life do-over, you will find these periods of retreat and reflection a welcome relief. Once you find your special place to visit and begin using your journal to record your ideas and inspirations, you will wonder what you ever did without this time for yourself and your life.

Revisit the Life Do-Over Strategies as Needed

I realize that each person who reads this book will be in a different place in life, with their own set of challenges and life experiences. Of the six life do-over strategies presented, certain ones will resonate deeply with some people, while different ones will ring true for others. As each person travels along their chosen life path, new issues will emerge along the way. That is why I encourage you to keep this book handy, and re-read the sections that speak to you at a particular time and place in your life.

For example, if you are overwhelmed and unable to find time for yourself, review Strategy #4 on how to make room for you in your life. If on the other hand, you feel a bit lost and confused and not sure of your path, re-read the ideas presented in Strategy #2 on how to connect with the real you, and Strategy #6 on how to listen to your wise, inner voice. Remember, once you think you have mastered these life do-over strategies, you will be presented with plenty of opportunities to demonstrate what you have learned. There is nothing wrong with taking an occasional refresher course and becoming reacquainted with the tools and techniques you find to be most helpful.

This is why I reread my favorite self-help and personal development books. I love to revisit and relearn the fundamental life strategies. So often, I think we mistakenly look for advanced theories about how to live our best lives. We forget that the advanced course comes from applying these basic concepts to our daily lives, and learning to live with more joy, ease, and fulfillment.

I encourage you to build a library of books that really speak to you and provide valuable resources for navigating your life path. To assist you in starting your collection, I have included as Appendix One a list of my favorite resources which you might find interesting. Please feel free to let me know if there is a resource you have found to be particularly useful. This is how I find new books to review in my newsletter and recommend to my clients. Plus, I can't help myself—receiving and sharing ideas is one of my gifts!

Develop a Life Do-Over Support System

Contemplating significant life changes can be an overwhelming process. While you may be very excited about the possibilities for your life, there will be days when you wonder if you really can chart a new course. This is when you'll want to be able to draw upon the support and guidance of positive, loving people who want what is best for you and/or have gone through a life do-over process themselves.

A great way to do this is to select a few friends and family members with whom you can share your dreams and desires. I did this while working as an attorney and beginning to explore my life do-over. I had several dear friends at work who would go for lunch or even a coffee break with me and let me share what I was feeling and thinking. Most of the time I wasn't really seeking answers from them, because I knew it was up to me to discover my own answers. They provided me with a safe place to express what was going on inside my head and heart, and to get various perspectives on my options. I am not sure I would have been able to finally summon the courage and resolve to forge a new life path without their support.

Now that I know about the profession of coaching, I can see that would have been the perfect time to work with a life coach. I didn't need a therapist. I was a whole, complete, healthy person who was at a major crossroads in life. I needed someone to assist me in clarifying what I really wanted to do and in developing an action plan for getting there. If you are in a similar place in life, consider working with a life coach. For more information about the process of life coaching, visit my website at www.cindyclemens.com. Another great resource is the International Coaching Federation, at www.coachfederation.org. You might even want to find out if anyone you know has worked with a life coach.

Enjoy the Journey

A natural tendency when we set our sights on a specific goal or destination is to get so focused on the outcome that we no longer enjoy the journey. We think all will be perfect if and when we get to a certain place in life. The problem with this mindset is that we miss out on the wonder of each day. We need to find a balance between creating a strategic plan for what we really want our lives to look and feel like, and being present to enjoy the precious moments of each day. The suggestions for resigning as Master of the Universe in Strategy #6 are my best ideas for how to achieve this balance.

This was my lesson to learn while on the yearlong RV trip. I kept reminding myself to enjoy the journey, work on whatever lessons presented themselves each day, connect with my wise, inner self, and let the ending unfold as it was supposed to. I did not want the days to go by in a blur of worry and anxiety about what we would decide to do with our lives at the end of the year. As a result, I can honestly say that the time did not fly by. The days were long and leisurely, and in the end, we were provided with the answers we had been seeking. I remind myself of this important lesson when I start worrying about how things will work out with my life coaching business.

Now that we are at the end of our time together, you are probably wondering how my life do-over has worked out. My answer is that I have absolutely no regrets about pursuing a new direction in life. I wake up each morning and am completely happy with how my day unfolds. I am no longer a slave to a rigid schedule set by others. Instead of solving problems and dealing with legal disputes, I am engaged in work that uses my gifts and fills my heart with passion. There is enough time during my day to take very good care of myself—I can take a brisk walk amidst the red rocks and desert scenery, play some afternoon golf, and even enjoy an occasional midday nap.

My business has developed so that it truly fits me and allows me to connect with interesting and inspiring clients and colleagues. Although I do have my occasional moments of fear and worry about how the income will show up each month, they don't last very long anymore. I know I am where I am supposed to be, doing what I am supposed to be doing, and I have a reserve of time and energy to enjoy it all. I consider my life do-over to be a great success!

I know that your life do-over will probably look very different from mine, and that is as it should be. You have different priorities, passions, and gifts to explore. You'll want your day to have a pace and rhythm that suits you. And the fears and doubts you'll need to overcome will be unique to you and your life experiences. What we do have in common, however, is a commitment to create our best lives—authentic lives that reflect what is most important to us and what we love to do.

In the final analysis, it is up to you to ask for a life do-over. No one can do it for you. And there is no time like the present to begin the journey. I wish you all the best and I send you love, laughter, and wisdom to help keep you on your path. Big hugs…

Go confidently in the direction of your dreams.
Live the life you always imagined.

—Henry David Thoreau

Appendix One

Additional Life Do-Over Resources

(These are the resources that I used during my life do-over, and continue to use today. When I feel myself getting off track or forgetting my way, I turn to the wisdom contained within theses books, daily readings, and oracle cards.)

BOOKS

- *A Return to Love*—Marianne Williamson

This book contains many of the pearls of wisdom from The Course in Miracles put into a context that is easy to grasp and apply to our everyday challenges. A great reminder of who we really are and what we are here to do.

- *Building Your Field of Dreams*—Mary Manin Morrissey

The author is a Unity minister, and in this book, she shares her own story of building a life full of joy, prosperity, and meaning. I discovered this gem early in my life do-over process, and its advice and support were invaluable in showing me the possibility of a new direction for my life.

- *Conversations With God: An Uncommon Dialogue* — Neale Donald Walsch

If you really want to open your mind to the possibility of a loving and accepting God, and move away from narrow, fundamentalist thinking, this is the book for you. But, be forewarned — it will shake up your paradigm and take you to a whole new level of spirituality.

- *Just Listen* — Nancy O'Hara

Whenever I tried to meditate and be still, I would struggle with quieting my mind. This book provided great exercises for how to be still and listen to the wise, inner voice, which was the key for me in accessing the wisdom of my real self.

- *Take Time for Your Life* – Cheryl Richardson

Not only is this the book that first introduced me to the profession of life coaching, but it showed me simple questions to ask myself and exercises to work through to have the time and energy for my life do-over.

- *The 11ᵗʰ Element* — Robert Scheinfeld

I actually discovered this book very recently, and it has become one of my favorites. The author provides a concrete and simple strategy for how to obtain guidance and resources from your internal CEO and the vast invisible network. Because it uses examples from the business world, it will appeal to those who would rather read business success books than self-help books.

- *The Joy Diet* — Martha Beck

I love the author's dry wit and humor, which come shining through in this delightful book about how to incorporate more joy into each day. I especially love the concept of treats — giving ourselves lots of treats every day to satisfy the inner beast.

- *The Mutant Message Down Under* — Marlo Morgan

This is an amazing tale of one woman's journey through the Australian Outback with a tribe of aborigines. The ancient wisdom, respect for nature, and trust in the abundance of Source demonstrated by these wise, loving people is a beautiful reminder of how we can live more simply and have more joy and ease. You won't be able to put it down. I reread it at least once a year.

- *The Power of Intention—Wayne Dyer*

I have enjoyed all of the author's many personal growth/spiritual connection books, and I think this one is his best. His insights into how we can connect with the creative power of Source and use the power of intentions to manifest whatever we want and need are so useful and powerful. I especially like the second portion of the book that applies the principles of intention to particular aspects of life, such as financial success, relationships, life purpose, and health.

- *The Seat of the Soul—Gary Zukav*

With the clarity and precision of a scientist's mind, the author explores how human beings are moving from being five-sensory beings to multi-sensory beings. He discusses the profound impact that is having, and will continue to have, on the evolution of human consciousness.

DAILY READINGS

Around the Year with Emmet Fox: A Book of Daily Readings—a collection of Emmet Fox's writings

Opening Doors Within: 365 Daily Meditations from Findhorn—Eileen Caddy

ORACLE CARDS

Healing with the Angels—Doreen Virtue

Appendix Two

My Journal
A Place to Start My Life Do-Over

Coepto Vita De Novo

Begin Life Anew

• Reflections from the Introduction •

How would I describe my path in life—in what direction am I headed? Is that where I want to be going?

What is working well in my life right now?

What is not working so well right now? What areas of my life are ready for a life do-over?

What questions from the Self-Assessment hit home with me?

What reasons am I giving myself as to why I cannot pursue a life do-over at this time? Are these valid reasons or expressions of fear?

What would my life do-over look like if I could get past those excuses and sources of resistance?

• Reflections on Strategy #1 •
Focus on Living from the Inside Out

The BE—DO—HAVE Model

• I want to BE

• From that, I want to DO

• Which will allow me to HAVE

• What is the cost of my stuff? Am I working to support my stuff? Is that OK? Am I really enjoying my stuff?

My self-discovery time

- When

- Where

- Alternative Locations

• Reflections on Strategy #2 •
Connect with My True Self

What is important to me?

- People

- Activities

- Lifestyle

- Personal Code of Conduct

What do I love to do?

- Activities about which I am passionate

- Possible indicators of my interests and passions

  ¤   Books

  ¤   News

  ¤   Movies

  ¤   People

- Three powerful questions

  ¤   What would I do if I absolutely, positively knew I would succeed?

  ¤   What would I do if I didn't have to worry about what others would think of my actions?

  ¤   What would I do if I knew I only had one year to live?

What am I meant to do—what are my special gifts and talents?

- What themes do I notice in my life?

- What can I not help myself from doing—what do I just do because it feels so natural and easy?

- What do people say I do for them?

- Start with my skills and talents—find the unique gifts underneath

- Phrasing my gift as a noun-verb combination

• Reflections on Strategy #3 •
Make Life Choices Consistent with My True Self

My YES List for right now in my life

What opportunities are showing up in my life and do they align with my YES List?

Why do I find it difficult to say NO?

What strategies can I use to make it easier to say NO without feeling guilty?

• Reflections on Strategy #4 •
Create Room for Me in My Life

Weekly Time Chart

	Mon	Tues	Wed	Thurs	Fri	Sat	Sun
6 a.m.							
7 a.m.							
8 a.m.							
9 a.m.							
10 a.m.							
11 a.m.							
Noon							
1 p.m.							
2 p.m.							
3 p.m.							
4 p.m.							
5 p.m.							
6 p.m.							
7 p.m.							
8 p.m.							
9 p.m.							
10 p.m.							
11 p.m.							
Midnight							
1 a.m.							
2 a.m.							
3 a.m.							
4 a.m.							
5 a.m.							

What does my Weekly Time Chart tell me about my time drains?

• Where am I wasting time? Let me consider the following questions

    ¤   Does this activity align with my YES List?

    ¤   Does this activity enhance my health or happiness?

    ¤   Does this activity really have to be done now or ever?

• How much of my time is spent caring for others? How much is spent caring for myself?

• Could I delegate and/or offload activities?

I am dealing with these energy vampires in my life

Energy Vampire #1 _____

Energy Vampire #2 _____

Energy Vampire #3 _____

- For Energy Vampire #1 — What is my strategy?

- For Energy Vampire #2 — What is my strategy?

- For Energy Vampire #3 — What is my strategy?

I want to take the Clutter Buster Challenge!

- I want to work on this area of clutter in my life

- I could eliminate this clutter by

  ¤ Option #1 —

  ¤ Option #2 —

  ¤ Option #3 —

- Specifically, my Clutter Buster Commitment is:

- I want to have a Clutter Buster partner!

  I will check-in with _____ by _____

  Phone or E-mail _____

These are the ways that I fill my internal energy tank

• Reflections on Strategy #5 •
Conquer My Fears and Doubts

Recognizing my fears

- What do they say?

- Whose voices do they use?

- When do they come—what time of day and which months?

My fear tool-kit

I can starve my fears by feeding my dreams—these are my dreams

Playing the "what-if" game

• The worst-case scenario that could happen is

• If this happened, what would happen next?

• And then what?

My Belief System — How the world works & the rules I accept as true

What is the failure story I tell myself when I don't reach my goals?

These are the doubts, negative self-talk, and limiting thoughts in my Belief System

- Do they have to be true for me?

- Do other people see things differently?

- What does the actual, concrete evidence in my life say about this belief?

• Reflections on Strategy #6 •
Resign as Master of the Universe

I want to try the following technique to help me resign as Master of the Universe and start having more joy and ease in my life

What I know to be true about this particular technique?

What I commit to doing this week so I can relax, enjoy the moments of my life, and take my hands off the steering wheel of life?

Success Tips for My Life Do-Over

My Resource List

My Support System

How I visualize my life do-over

- Physical Environment

- Daily Flow

- People

- Type of Work

- Free Time Pursuits

Acknowledgements

This book would not have been possible without the ideas and inspiration I received from my clients, workshop and retreat participants, and newsletter readers. Thank you for all you have given me and for your generosity of spirit. I love learning with you!

I would like to acknowledge a few special people by name. To my wonderful family, Steve and Jan Bohrer, Lynn Abercrombie, Tracy Bohrer, and all of the Clemens clan, I value your love and support so much. You never seem to falter in your support and belief in me. This is doubly true of my husband and best friend, Jim.

To my reading and editing team, thanks to Carol Golichnik, Michelle Bridges, Jane Miner, and Kayla Koeber. Your feedback and suggestions provided just the right polish for the book.

A special thanks to my publishing angels – Lana Jordan and Jill Ronsley at Jorlan Publishing, who guided me through the publishing process, and Paula Leckey, who created the beautiful front cover design.

And finally, to all the friends and colleagues who supported me during my life do-over, thank you for your friendship and wisdom. I could not have made it to this point if you had not been there in the beginning. Especially, thanks to Jeff Jorgensen, Sharon Woodward, Sue Baasch, Jill Sylvain, Wendy George, and Judith Propp

May you continue to explore and enjoy new paths in life!

About the Author

Cindy has traveled an interesting path on her way to becoming a life coach, author, and motivational speaker. After graduating from Occidental College in 1982 with a bachelor's degree in political science, Cindy attended Hastings College of Law and graduated in 1985 with her juris doctorate. Sworn in as a member of the California State Bar in 1985, she began her legal career as a criminal prosecutor and appellate attorney.

In 1990, Cindy and her husband, Jim, moved to the central coast of California, where Cindy worked as an in-house municipal attorney and became involved in the San Luis Obispo Community Theater, acting in several productions.

In 1998, Cindy realized that she was ready for some significant life changes. No longer fulfilled by the practice of law, she could feel the winds of change blowing. While enjoying an extended cross-country RV trip, Cindy serendipitously discovered the profession of life coaching and knew this would be her new career. After graduating from the two-year training program at Coach U, the final piece fell into place when she found her new home amidst the spectacular red rocks and mountains of southern Utah.

Cindy feels so fortunate to have created a life that combines her passion for personal growth with her talent for connecting with people and inspiring them to live their best lives. Cindy offers individual and group coaching programs, life strategy workshops, and engaging motivational talks.

You can find out more at www.cindyclemens.com.